# QUESTIONS OF LOVE

Also by Rika Lesser

Poetry

*Etruscan Things*, 1983
*All We Need of Hell*, 1995
*Growing Back: Poems 1972-1992*, 1997

Poetry in Translation

*Holding Out* (Poems of Rainer Maria Rilke), 1975
*Hours in the Garden and Other Poems* by Hermann Hesse, 1979
*Guide to the Underworld* by Gunnar Ekelöf, 1980
*Rilke: Between Roots*, 1986
*A Child Is Not a Knife: Selected Poems of Göran Sonnevi*, 1993
*What Became Words: Poems* by Claes Andersson, 1996
*Siddhartha: An Indic Poem* by Hermann Hesse, 2007

Selected Prose Retellings & Translations

*Hansel and Gretel* (Illustrated by Paul O. Zelinsky), 1984
*A Living Soul* by P C Jersild, 1988
*A Hand Full of Stars* by Rafik Schami, 1990
*Agnes Cecilia* by Maria Gripe, 1990
*My Sister Lotta and Me* (Text by Helena Dahlbäck, Pictures
    by Charlotte Ramel), 1993

# QUESTIONS OF LOVE

## NEW & SELECTED POEMS

## RIKA LESSER

The Sheep Meadow Press
Riverdale-on-Hudson, New York

Designed and typeset by The Sheep Meadow Press
Distributed by The University Press of New England

All inquiries and permission requests should be addressed to the publisher:

The Sheep Meadow Press
PO Box 1345
Riverdale, NY 10471

Cover image: *Leda and the Swan* by Lelio Orsi

Library of Congress Cataloging-in-Publication Data

Lesser, Rika.
  Questions of love : new & selected poems / Rika Lesser.
      p. cm.
  Includes bibliographical references.
  ISBN 1-931357-60-9
  I. Title.
  PS3562.E837Q47 2008
  811'.54--dc22

                                        2008020339

# Acknowledgments

Grateful acknowledgment is made to the editors and publishers of journals and books in which a number of these poems have appeared, sometimes in different forms, as noted below.

**QUESTIONS OF LOVE**
*Barrow Street*: "Around Midnight"
*Caprice*: "Surviving Parent"
*Heliotrope* (print & online): "To Autumn"
*Knockout*: "QUESTIONS OF LOVE, RECONSIDERED: VII. Shift"
*Literary Imagination*: "Coronation"
*Manhattan Review*: "With Poppies"
*New Letters:* "In a Bottle" and "Standing Meditation"
*Pequod*: "At the Sea" and "*The Ice, The Road, The Hedge*"
*Pleiades*: "Operation"
*Ploughshares*: "Possession"
*Provincetown Arts*: "QUESTIONS OF LOVE, RECONSIDERED: IV. Solitude, V. Thirst"
*The Paris Review*: "Daddy's Girl"
*The St. Ann's Review*: "Second Childhood"
*Taiga*: "QUESTIONS OF LOVE, RECONSIDERED: Prologue: On Love, I. Falling, II. Taking Sides, III. Later"
"About Her" first appeared in *Poetry* (August 1997); it was reprinted in *Best American Poetry 1998*.
"*Opposite Corners*" was commissioned for *Words for Images: A Gallery of Poems*, edited by John Hollander and Joanna Weber, Yale University Press, 2001.
"Operation" appeared in a doctoral study, *Lena Cronqvist: Reflections of Girls* by Katarina Wadstein MacLeod (Malmö: Sekel, 2006).
"Self-Portraits: Reflections" was commissioned for the catalogue *Lena Cronqvist: Self-Portraits and Girls, Paintings, Sculptures, and Prints* October 19 – December 9, 2006 (Nancy Margolis Gallery, 2006).

**SELECTED POEMS**
*Pleiades*: "Let's throw it out the window"
*Poetry*: "Translation" and "Losses"
*The New Yorker*: "527 Cathedral Parkway"

Poems first collected in *All We Need of Hell* appear with the kind permission of the University of North Texas Press: "The Room," "BLACK STONES I," "BLACK STONES IV: (First Sight)," "BLACK STONES VI: (Falling)," "Matthew's Passion," "BLACK STONES VIII: (And were You lost, I would be—)," "White Stone," "Love," "BLACK STONES XII: (Care)," "For Elisabeth," "BLACK STONES XIV," "The Other Life," and "September '92: Measures."

Poems first collected in *Growing Back: Poems 1972-1992* appear with the kind permission of the University of South Carolina Press: "Translation," "Losses," "Værøy," "Growing Back," "The Gifts," "Lyric," "Departures," "536 Saratoga Avenue," "Under the Roof," "527 Cathedral Parkway," "Ein Gebliebtes: The Body of the Work," "The News & The Weather," "PAGES TOWARD THE TURN OF THE YEAR," "CAN ZONE or THE GOOD FOOD GUIDE."

Poems in **ETRUSCAN THINGS** were originally published in a book by that title in the Braziller Series of Poetry in 1983.

# Contents

## QUESTIONS OF LOVE

## SELECTED POEMS

### FIRST POEMS: 1972–1974

### BLUEPRINTS AND MONUMENTS: 1974–1983

# QUESTIONS OF LOVE

In memory of my sister Fran Robin Lesser

(7 August 1948 – 23 December 2003)

The memory of this face among other faces
will follow me, I will carry it
with me, within me, always. . . .

Gunnar Ekelöf

# QUESTIONS OF LOVE, RECONSIDERED

Loving in truth, and fain my love in verse to show,
. . . . . . . . . . . . . . . . . . . . . . . . . . . . .
But words came halting out, wanting invention's stay,
Invention, Nature's child, fled Stepdame Study's blows:
And others' feet still seemed but strangers in my way
Thus great with child to speak, and helpless in my throes,
    Biting my tongue and pen, beating my self for spite:
    Fool, said my muse to me, look in thy heart and write.


—Sir Philip Sidney

## Prologue: On Love

Need for a new start, a new love, a new
project  Continuing work  Questions go
on and on  An old love returned (not re-
quited), returning, come back, out of
nowhere (it seemed) one day  From the vapors,
from cyberspace, a cypher, a gesture:
one hand scooped his hair out of his eyes in-
cessantly  All I could recall  He claimed
to remember much more  That I sang to
him, stroked his thigh  What do I know or want
Everything  Nothing  Compassion  Connec-
tedness I rarely feel, except with—now
say it, Girl—except with say, minerals,
except with, say, cycles  WHAT CAN I GIVE?

## I. Falling

WHO FELL? WHO'S FALLING? WHERE? HEAD OVER
HEELS? HEEDING WHAT HEALS? HEALING WHO HEEDS?

LOVESICK? Nightbird   Next day risen   Night-
owl   Heartsick   Heart heavy (or light)   Sus-
pended, hanging in a balance be-
tween love and the work   *His* love, for she
grows dearer to him by the stroke; he
thanks her   FOR SPENDING THE TIME?   WHO FLIES?

DOES HE KNOW HOW FRAGILE IT IS?—WHAT
EVER IS BETWEEN THEM—HOW HIS TONE,
DESCENDS LIKE A BOULDER, WITHOUT IN-
TENDING TO, CUTS LIKE A KNIFE   Today
she woke thinking, repeating once more
to herself: *Go now, go, go on*   Were
he to fall desperately, she'd turn
the other way

## II. Taking Sides

Where is she really?   Not *in love* but
loving   Even attached (limpet or
barnacle?)   Feet planted, maybe not
down to earth or tongue in groove   Though she
is labile, not liable to fall   What
if she settled?—here or there, her mind,
for him?   Yes, what if?

                    And what about
him?   On the far side of an ocean,
working, working away   Can life be
his focus?   What about the kids he
wants to have?   (May be too old to have)
Who knows?

             She wants none, never has at
any age   Nowadays still could have
at the risk (off meds, if she didn't
want a monster) of *her* own life   But
if he can't love, love *her* enough, how
then love a child?

                How hurt he must have
been, must be, how frail, never ever
to say *I love*

## III.  Later

He says it
just in time
to keep her—at least
for a time   Now
without seeing it
she lets herself
fall   Doesn't know
till afterward   Too
late   Again he's
gone   *This* time is
not limited
                    He
says it again: *Lots
of love* he
cries from a
distance
              His
father has died
(Hers died years ago)
More than ever
he wants to be
one   More
than ever she
is alone

## IV. Solitude

Come home to roost?
Where did that come
from?  Old English
*hróst*: a perch, a
roof spar, a bird's
resting place (not
a nest) related
to palate (whose
origin may
be Etruscan)
The mouth-roof, the
mind goes far afield

Back in her own mouth
Eating her words   Tired
Sick and tired   No
longer sick   Unafraid
of what the illness
may do to her or
she to herself
*Semper parata*,
always conscious,
always on guard, though
more discreetly now
Tired of what she sees
and hears all around
her, less and less sure
how to move on   She
pauses,  reflects:

*There's someone I*
*love   Someone I*

*did love   Now pushed*
*to the side   All*
*in abeyance*
*(Old French* bayer*:*
*to open the*
*mouth wide)   His words*
*are few   His tone*
*cheerful, cruel*
*His need—if not*
*desperate—severe*
*MINE?   I've been here*
*before, resting*
*unquiet beneath*
*a thin blanket,*
*heeding voices*
*under this roof*

*Our time here to-*
*gether changes*
*nothing that came*
*before   DID IT*
*HELP US TO TAKE*
*IN MORE?*
                    *YOU*
*WHO BELIEVE IN*
*THE SOUL, TELL ME*
*HOW MUCH DAILY*
*ENMESHMENT LOVE*
*NEEDS TO EXACT*
*MUST LOVERS BE*
*PHYSICALLY*
*PRESENT?   ONCE LOVE*
*HAS TAKEN A*
*HEART, WHAT DOES IT*
*GIVE BACK?*

## V. Thirst

Love's not a stream
but a faucet
one of her friends
attests   It runs
hot or cold, turns
on and off  WHO'S
IN CONTROL THEN
she wonders  GOD
THE PLUMBER? *Drought*
*is still drought*
         *ISN'T*
*IT BETTER: WALKING*
*BY THE SEA ALONE*
*THAN TRYING TO PRESS*
*WATER FROM A STONE*

## VI. Players

I want to speak to you
I will have to write of you
And about betrayal
The sense I may always be
betrayed—*disappointed?*—
fail to be properly
appreciated when I
have not failed in my task but
fail to be preferred for
some other reason to some
other person or thing

Not playing the game  (WHY SHOULD
I?  WAS I EVER A CHILD?)
Not in the schoolyard where
the boys were noisy and rough
(WHERE WERE THE OTHER GIRLS?)
WHY COMPETE?  WHY DEMAND
A REWARD?  WHAT DOES ONE
TRULY WANT?  One wants to
be noticed   One wants to
be loved, vocally
and forever

       Again, Love,
you have gone where I can't
reach you   This is *your* life
choice:  an attempt to control
all ties   I can live without
you   I have for years   We both
know your silence is cruel   HOW
TO REPAY YOU IN KIND?   Now

you must play by my rule:
*It's not enough to act with-*
*out malice aforethought when*
*you know how to do no harm*

## VII. Shift

Now that we've settled—
or things have shaken out
separating into
a different pattern—
it's time to reflect,
to refract differently
on our past, our pasts, our re-
pasts   Only yesterday when
I passed the Garden of Eden
on Montague Street, my mind's
eye streamed, seeing the goose
you cooked for us last Christmas
My first   I bought a small potted
pine, and we had gingerbread
ornaments, Sacher Torte, a plum
pudding you flamed and served
with brandy butter to me and
fellow Jews. . . . Did we fight that day?
More than likely   Our pattern
then
       Who would not wonder,
one bleak day in the fall, one
parent gone, the other be-
ginning to go, if something
else were not possible

## VIII.  To Love Now


You say I don't look back
don't turn to wave when we
part, when *I* leave

                  (That's how
it is—so you've made me
believe—the set-up, you
unable to come here
where I live, where I love
living   Believe it or
not, I love this city,
the state of it)
              Today
you spoke of using the
pronoun we
          in future


Still in the present, some-
where my sister taught me
to be while she was dying:


       I'm walking down Houston
       to MacDougal, turning
       without looking, the light
       changing with me, the wind
       blowing   A man with his
       obstreperous German
       shepherd yells at tourists
       who don't yield the right of
       way: *Been here 50 years,*
       *but don't make a path for*
       *me, 50 years before*
       *you, don't bother!*  On my

way home:  past Film Forum's
Bergman Festival and
a film by Lars von Trier
Nothing's ever dubbed there

(Of course I'm not in the
present   This all happened
earlier   By the time
you read this, days, weeks, months,
years have passed)

                    Walking,
thinking how vulnerable
I am now   To love YOURS
ALONE? . . .

                You mentioned ex-
ploring Vienna's ex-
pat community   I
fell silent   Protected
from you by my mother
until she dies   From your
offer to part me from
my life as I've known it

WHAT HAS YOUR LOVE TAUGHT ME
IN ITS DESIRE FOR FULL-
TIME PRESENCE, ATTENTION
IF NOT POSSESSION:—?

> *Where is a man who has the right to possess?*
> *Who can possess what does not hold itself,*
> *what only from time to time blissfully catches itself*
> *and throws itself again. Like a child a ball. . . .*

                    Good
old Rilke  ARE MEN AND
WOMEN SO DIFFERENT?
The ball is in both courts

## IX.  Break Time

*Third week in August*

Here we are again   Again "finding
ourselves" on both sides, on either side
of a di*vide* (WERE WE EVER ONE?—
seems that second syllable goes back
to Sanskrit *vindhate*: he lacks) an
ocean neither of us sees filled with
possibility   ARE WE TOO OLD
FOR THAT? TOO DUMB?
                    Taking care again—
now it is my mother whose decline
grows more precipitous—I phone you
as my day ends, hot tears welling up,
washing my voice, breaking your day, break-
ing into it, the ice of your voice,
your temperament  You turn over in
bed, all elbows   I weep profoundly
excuse myself, hang up the phone  You
call back, read to me, breathe me to sleep

*Near September eleventh*

At a quarter to one in my morning, on
the road, the European road between your
sense of community (near Augsburg) and your
sense of home (in Wien) you phone me on what you
call a "mobile" and I a "cell"  The surprise—
your voice goes wooden, hollow, gnarled, apolo-
gizing for some meaninglessness someone else
might laugh off—turns to shock:
                    *Give us a rest*
                    you ask   And I

answer: There's no
such thing as mo-
tionlessness   I
sleep like the dead
but am no good
at keeping still
on urgencies
Matters of the
heart demand re-
sponse:  libations—
tears or blood—are
vows that flow, for
me, from the lips
open-hearted
open-mouthed  A
commitment could
hurl one or both
of us every-
where all at once
A REST?  Silence
means Death  To me
Caesurae—come
where they may:  mid-
foot, mid-verse, mid-
melody, choose
your white frame of
reference—are
cut-offs, stops  You
pause, go on   They
don't invite re-
pose
        You say I've
"made something of
my life"  I still
want love

                    Love, you
long have had the
benefit of
mine   Wanting yours—
evidence there-
of—I'm afraid
we've reached the end
                    of the line

## X. *An den fernen Geliebten* or Care, Revisited


It's odd, truly odd (Ekelöf held that the
number of life was odd, that of death
even) our latest *tvist* over words:  where
there are two, there will be (if the two are
we) not contentment but contention  You
and I allegedly speak the same language
Nevertheless, our Englishes seem a pair
of long stiff gloves, hardly fit to be tied
When we talk about what we "want most from"
a "life" partner, you invoke *contribution*,
I *support*
           How shall I take your word?


Any way I look, your word's concern is
giving to a common fund or store,
voluntarily or not  What do we
ultimately own? Our bodies? You
must know under early English law a pledge
was a person whose body was given
as security for the performance
of an obligation, what we now call
a *hostage*  Contribution: *mutual
tribute?*—howsoever paid, that ac-
knowledges submission   I'm afraid,
at bottom, with the brightest that fell, I
still assert: *Non serviam*
                Dear heart,
there will be no romantic poems written
about us, no romances, indeed no
romanzero  Not by me, not by you,
that's clear  Though we exchange words on machines
that are penetrable, pregnable

even, to others; *who*—as you might say—
*at the end of the day*, you might ask, *who cares?*

Care is my watchword, again, as ever   For
the living and the dead, the great enigma
we encounter on paths to the half-finished
heaven—to borrow titles from Tranströmer
rather than Heine   To look back on my own
BLACK STONES XII, *its* sorrow   Here I am, again,
as ever, mourning my sister, watching my
mother go far more slowly

                         When I can't bear,
cannot endure something alone, I want *sup-*
*port*, help from below with the portage,
the passage, the faring, *translation* itself

In other words: Understanding, the sense
you stand beside me wherever you may be
Not literally feeding me, like a stream, a
tributary   Not legs and footsoles, not wall,
chair, bolster, brace, no *Famille de saltimbanques*
standing there in place to form the initial
D of *Dastehen* on a lost *Teppich im*
*Weltall*: cosmic carpet, metaphorical,
worn threadbare from the eternal rehearsal
of acrobatic moves by—WHOM? WHO *ARE*
MORE FLEETING THAN WE?

                        MIGHT LUCIFER BE
OUR ANGEL? CAN YOU HOLD ME IN YOUR
HEART-SPACE WITH ROOM TO SPARE? MIGHT WE BE THAT
ONCE MISMATCHED PAIR, WHOSE HEARTS *CAN* NOW PERFORM
VAULTING FEATS, WHO STAND AS LADDERS, ON NOTHING,
NO COMMON GROUND, LEANING ONLY AGAINST
EACH OTHER, TREMBLING, SMILING GENUINELY
ON THE SOOTHED CARPET   TO WHOM THE COUNTLESS,

SILENT DEAD FINALLY TOSS THEIR FOREVER
HOARDED, FOREVER HIDDEN, ETERNALLY
VALID COINS OF FORTUNE, NOWHERE IN
OUR KEN

## XI. *Unheimlich*

You had me when
you wanted me
Then you didn't
any longer

Sorry you kept
saying
          Sorry
first and last word
out of your mouth

I had used words:
*reject    betray
responsibility*
You kept saying
sorry   Sorry
to disappoint
Kept speaking of
boarding school

Yes it must be
very different:
being stashed a-
way from home   A
light shines on you
when a parent
comes to visit
Then you revert
to a world of
other children
and *their* games

When not in school
I was kept in
mostly, where I
might be seen or
vaguely heard by
parents barely
there, registered
as present   I had
to create my
own world without
any other
children—my sisters
grew older—make
up my own games

And so I made
this path, this frame-
work, this house in
which to live a
life without some-
one else's god
Matter enough
Spirit aplenty

You set yourself
in my path, de-
manding: *Love me*
Child, I did   Then

you walked away

## XII. Quartet

### I. Love

We still can't say what it is
yet want it desperately
each of us from the other
Or, maybe not, maybe just
from someone, anyone
who will stay near—or keep
a distance
         For some time
quite a long time this time
I thought it possible
An arrangement between us:
half the year here, half there, of
separate necessities
not always together

### II. Syncopated Clocks

So many words uttered when we first met
again less than three years ago
echo: "You can see as much of me as
you like. . . . I can't sustain this long
distance"  About most things you mainly told
the truth all too sparingly   I
stood incredulous: a man who hated
my birthplace without faithfully
living here, memorizing a painting
at the Met: "I may never come
back"  You left two years ago, knowing you'd
make no effort to  YOU LOVE ME?
WHAT ON EARTH CAN I SAY?  Look me up if
you find yourself back in New York someday—

## III. Life & Death

DEAR RAINER, OLD MASTER I ADHERED TO WHEN,
AT EIGHTEEN, I OUTGREW HESSE . . . THOUGH NOW I'VE
OUTLIVED YOU BY HALF A YEAR AND PAULA BY
TWO DECADES, WILL I EVER GET PAST YOU TWO?

> *Wir haben, wo wir lieben, ja nur dies:*
> *einander lassen; denn daß wir uns halten,*
> *das fällt uns leicht und ist nicht erst zu lernen.*

> We have where we love only this:
> to release each other, for to hold one another
> comes easily to us and need not be learned.

("Requiem"; translation mine, of course)   Had you
wed Paula Becker and not Clara Westhoff
that would have changed the whole course . . .

## IV. Careless Love

Distant Love, carelessly apart for thirty
years, you and I still live, still live well
apart   Neither of us can easily let
go of the vestige, the concept, not
even in the other's absence   Is
ANYTHING TRUE ABOUT TRUE LOVE?
WHOM DO I QUIETLY BETRAY
ASKING FAR TOO MANY QUESTIONS?
WHAT SEEMS IMPOSSIBLE NOW, TODAY?

> MAYBE NEITHER OF US EVER REALLY FELL
> IF I WAS ABOUT TO, DID I WANT TO BE
> CAUGHT AND RIGHTED AND MOVE ON?   OR HELD
> IN PLACE, TO ROOT, BRANCH, FLOWER, FAIL

## Envoy:  Christmas Present, 2005

Now at the darkest time
you bring me
darkness, old lover   No,
old love who
never loved me   You bring me
tidings, not
glad ones, joy  Nothing new
just old news
You ask me to recall
a death I
cannot forget, and to
ritualize it
as *you* would   Thank you,
no
     You will deny
my pain, my joy—con-
tinually
as you always did
from the first day
            I
did not recognize
your face in
your mirror   Or why you
smelled so sweet
I was simply drugged   All
right, seduced—

Harshly you questioned how I ever
could involve myself with an Arab
who declaimed his love for me

repeatedly, lived here with me and
knew me, finally, no better than
you did   COULD I BELIEVE *HIM*?

                              Label it
weakness   Call it tolerance    He took
from me back then—so much less myself
ten years ago than now—no more,  no less
than you still try to

## ABOUT HER

"Hamlet" to Himself were Hamlet—
Had not Shakespeare wrote—
Though the "Romeo" left no Record
Of his Juliet,

It were infinite enacted
In the Human Heart—
Only Theatre recorded
Owner cannot shut—

—Emily Dickinson

## About Her

### I. At sixes and sevens

What I cannot remember
about that day that time
was simply gone   (*Simply? A*
*drop from a height, a blow*
*to the head, made my brain whirl*)
Comes calling now—Lost Soul—
to haunt   Lost twin I longed for
all the days of my life
Long gray afternoons we played
together, made up songs
drew, read books   She and I
identical
             (*And lethal*)


I did not know her power
where she came from, how she got
so strong   It seems she came one
day when I was thirty-one
Came with the illness to take
care of me   Take these pills she'd
say, a lot of pills   How changed
she was! Knowing better than
I what could not be taken:
The intolerable: Life
a cul-de-sac
             Then *she* was


gone seven years   My flesh
my blood   I did not know
her, recognize her tread

Wiser, she knew where to
keep hid   Nearly a year
she lived invisibly
Out of thin air one day
she took me over   Where?

                         No

matter   My trust was a
sister's trust—the youngest—
unaware sisterhood
is sometimes murderous

## II. Rrrrose

She hates me wants to see me dead and stops
at nothing—mimics taunts and jeers, wielding
the lines of my palm, wearing my clothes
this twin   The girl I never was

> *Name her   Turn on light after light*
> *Sharply limned, first she will split*
> *then burn beneath your mind's focus*

An old French teacher—hairy legs, seamed hose—
in what? 8th grade? insisted I was Rrrrose
My own first name unutterable she said
in *that* language   I couldn't breathe   Instead
turned up my nose, took a tropistic turn
toward the midnight sun—first via German—
where, guttural or trilled initially,
R could exist and flourish and be me

I want to believe I am not alone
without *her*   That there exists some Other
with a different mien—not smirking
not looking blankly on as I drop down

and down   Be she Sister, Healer, or Some-
one in my image, who comes through the mirror

## III.   Reproduction

Is she *ma mort*, the one whose gloves cut
through the mirror?  Cocteau's Princess—
no queen—just another messenger
poets want to take for their own
Death?
        Is she minute, a seed still green
and "warm with night, dug from the soil-
bed of *my* heart, from which *my* Death shall
germinate"?  Will I like Paula
Becker "eat its kernels"?
                Childless by
choice, neither do I want to take
death in *and* bear it, nor walk pregnant
into the afterlife


                Sister,
spit and image, there is so little
we rule: The forces of Fate are
steadfast   Death adheres to the fertile
Kore's chastity did not save her
The choice was narrow and costly: Shun
the strange red fruit or patiently
wander the underworld forever

"Let us mourn together" Rilke
wrote in his Requiem for Paula
"that someone took you out of your
mirror"  For now she would paint no more—
no more portraits, fruits, self-portraits
with amber beads—leaving nothing

behind but mourners

                    (*Her child lived*)


Does it all start in the mirror, *der*
*Spiegel*, the noun of looking and
seeing, the pool of self-hate and self-
love, reflecting all things evil
and good?  Did Narcissus see in the
water a beloved dead twin
sister?
          Do all our makings go on
there, not through the window but in
the mirror?  And if so, can you help
me?  Sister?

## Surviving Parent

In memory of my father Milton S. Lesser (1914-1998)


My mother returns, gives herself up
to the weather, saying:
—It is so bright, I feel so
well, the sky is *blue*!

     My mother recedes, walks
     through a door of darkness
     like a man in a Bacon canvas
     mostly black

She's losing us, whom she
carried, slowly losing
her grasp   Her memory
is going, I will not say
her *mind*  We try to hold her
She will not be consoled

     My mother recedes
     gives herself up to darkness
     at times   This we share—
     just we two: the issuing
     in and out of darkness
     advancing in and out of us:
     a wave now damped
     now amplified

          Now I live elsewhere,
          give myself up to the language
          Which has changed me,
          changed for me, changed itself
               (as language will do)

Fluency shifts, drags when the water
runs high   Words grow thick
in my mouth   My ear cups them,
seines them, serves them up
in neither language   Hollow,
I mimic my mother  (*We
speak across seas in just one
language*)  take nothing in

Mother returns   Each day
is like a new penny
shiny and bright   When she
comes through the door the light
I imagine around her
is blinding

Blinded by tears as well,
whom do I weep for now
For her, being here, per-
haps no more partially
than ever   For him, being
gone a year or more

When it comes to the heart—
my father taught—
silence reigns

*Stockholm, 1999*

## *Opposite Corners*

after Sylvia Plimack Mangold

### I. Edginess

In the one opposite,
if mirrors can be believed,
we've passed or gone through (*bro-
ken's* too jagged a word) the look-in-
glass and are in that room
behind the mirror

                    Or else the room zig-
zags   Or else a squared pillar—of Flame *at the
White Heat?*—congeals in the opposite corner

      The room is empty
      thus you are not there
      but should be

      A third eye hovers
      well above the frame
      reckoning with
      perspectives  (*Which
      calipers?  Whose rules?*)

Reason's not reason enough
that the painting—and it is a painting,
very much a painting about painting—
appeals to me, poet, maker, shaper
that I am

## II.  Disappearance

Is this how we look inside: empty and
unimaginable, and clean?
Full of reflective—self-reflexive?—tricks
vistas that open but do not exist?
My portrait!
Cover the mirror, there has been a death
Unveil the mirror   *Just let go the Breath*
into the glass   Your absence—conspicuous
Empty everything out impulsively
Empty everything out but carefully
Can one be too careful—too serious?
Both possible and real: this Emptiness
Time to clear out
Words grow too heavy for us

## III.  Sight Unseen

I view your canvas after my father's death:
How different in the flesh!  Closer to square!
A pale gray shadow broods over the mirror
on a white abyss cropped from the photograph
The floor a sea of planks, pine more gold than red,
on which a lustrous trapezoid floats, listing
to the left   Above the baseboard the paint dips,
the mark of masking tape?  In the glass one board
collects a burnished drip of acrylic paint
I think I see a ghost, an afterimage,
a mote in the eye, a gleam—a bare hint of
the opposite corner in the floor's high sheen
      You worked on this painting
      three years earlier than
      a seminal drawing
      in your own collection:

*With a Vanishing Point*
*of 66″*
where two metal rulers,
both so-called *EXACT*, pro-
pagate others—a field
of more abstract measures,
inscribed for your father,
"diminished at 66"

Call this *Mourning and Marginalia*
Call it *Crossing the Styx:*
    Emptiness clear, a gas
    expanding   Emptiness
    ordered, composition
    extending   Into what
    we don't know, cannot
    ever know   Now turn
    the page, go on   *Release*
    the soul

## Around Midnight

for Fran


My sister has death on her plate
She eats heartily  She eats well
Her eyes are wide   Are sad   Immersed
in confusion, not in much pain
(physical pain), her time is short

My mother's plate is clean   Her mind
is blank, but she still knows us   Sweet-
tempered as she never was   Her
time seems boundless   This is not fair
What is the force that keeps her here?

Where did I write those words I
cannot find now?  What matters
is what we leave behind   Is
what matters what we leave   What
is matter?  All that we leave?
Behind us:  all we have left
All those we have left without
knowing   Without our knowledge
(*What kind?*)
                    What did we know as
children that we do not now?
Forgotten?  Denied?  Suppressed?
In every sense:  Lost

My sister asks: *Where is my
knowledge?*  I tell her I know
how she feels   A lie   I know
how it feels to wait to be
"well" on a far slower course
of an illness that's incurable

I listen to Mahler, to
his *Kindertotenlieder*
and the other Rückert Lieder
We were children, and we are
older children now, and we are
dying, Fran, you especially
much too fast

*17/18 December 2003*

## Second Childhood

I visit my mother
nowadays she is younger,
harder to focus, more
distant, sweeter   I feed her
plain Hershey's milk chocolate
nuggets   She prefers these to
all forms of Lindt, Droste,
Fazer Blue (the only *milk*
chocolate I'd eat for years)
Today I could not get her
to see the woodpecker—
black and white with one red patch
on his head—on the sole
pine trunk some yards ahead of
her   Could she not look up?
Was the sky too bright to look
into?  The distance itself?
The radiance glaring
off her cataracts, which she
still reads through—if you ask
her, or guide her
                              *Didn't*
*Daddy* (*my* father) *make you*
*look at birds?*  (He recorded
his sightings, their songs)   *Daddy,*
*never* . . . she pauses   We may
well not be talking about
the same man

## To Autumn

I wanted both my parents to die
together   They did not oblige me

though they formed *the parental unit*
all *my* life   Now my mother has out-
lived it more than seven years, as my
eldest sister & I approach our
middle sister's second yahrzeit—or
it us—as days shorten, reds deepen
She knows us, Mother; when prompted re-
members Milton, Fran   How long would he
have survived the loss of her?   And her
losses?

Last week I may have saved my mother's
life—I owe her my own many times
over   An *antibiotic* she
is *sensitive* (read: allergic) to
was prescribed and fed to her once or
twice (Think positive: Mithridates,
eating poisons, to build tolerance,
become immune)   I put an end to
that "mistake"   Dying *now* is not her
choice   Nor mine for her to make   I want
my mother to die in her sleep
                      Where
would you have yours die?
                      And by what
means?

# THE GIRLS

after Lena Cronqvist

## To Lena

What we have behind us has the same
fundamental, the same prime tone   Need
we call it psychosis   Some other
term   Experience, then   Who we are,
what we've been through and done   How we go
on, both with life and with art: careful
or reckless or both   No other choice

Your girls now are mine—I typed *mind* (are
being mined)   Now that you're done with them
(or soon may be) you have given them
to me as you have to everyone
All along you and I have learned
trust

     Could I manage paints and a brush
this whole enterprise would be other-
wise   Between us: wordlessness, color,
image, insertion, response   You, my
friend, publicly taciturn, ask if
I have questions   What shall I ask you

## Possession

Whose girls are these,
yours, mine, ours, everyone's?
So many deny them
*(Oh, no, not more of those!)*
Often your sister
Sometimes another girl
Always your parents
(For me dark is normal)

Is it conceivable
your parents or my own
actually could have done
anything deserving
of how the girls treat them?

> In a glass bubble—
> one to each figure-
> head—more balloon than
> retort, old Mom or Dad
> twist and turn, wave stumps of
> arms, press the glass with their
> hands, shouting or shrieking—
> air supply gone
> > The girls
> look delighted   Whose-
> ever they are

Ours, our sisters, blond
or not, with or without
braids or bows, younger or
older   They play   They learn
cruelty   They—this is
hard to see—are learning
love

## At the Sea

These girls have backbone   Always
stand straight   No matter what goes
down or lies before them   Though
they may bend, they don't break   No
matter how black the shades of
their parents in front, in back

Now and then hand in hand, in
the sea they'll wade or sit down
and play, each with her doll or
cat or bear   Their sex smooth and
white, exposed, without a hair
Now the older (Lena, that's
you), on the verge of a rage,
tries to submerge the younger
girl, who grabs the blue water
like a chink in a wall

## The Ice, The Road, The Hedge

How dark they are
these parents in
their coats: Black   Black-
gray, brownish   Black-
green   Their faces
gray, dark blue, and
black again   No-
where white, not in
their eyes   Thick coats
of darkness   All
expressionless

No matter the
season, you and
Kerstin are light
In winter in
*The Ice*: Your white
skin, red bow, her
white cap   An ice-
bound lake behind
you meets the sky
Little contact,
though she takes your
mother's hand   Your
dad—broad, shoulders
squared, arms frozen
to his sides—stands
isolate

In *The Road* your
little sister
stands alone, still

flanked, in tears, arms
flailing, as if
she'd just learned to
walk   Her golden
yellow costume
(the one she got
and you did not—
no happier
for that) touches
the ground   The road
extends behind
her   Red roses
strewn on her cap,
her collar; an
apron, long and
white, obscures her
feet

      On your side
of *The Hedge* that's
severing you
and your mom from
Dad, it's summer
Mother wears a
gray dress   You, bare-
legged, thrust your
bare chest forward
above a short
skirt covered with
polka dots   Your
hands, palms up, cup
treasures from the
soil   Father, still
in a topcoat
and wide-brimmed hat,

peers down at you,
strangely smiles
The hedge's rose–
madder branches
stretch upward, black–
ened flames
                You look
away, farther,
farther away

# Daddy's Girl

Does she feel safe there, between her dad's
big knees   She stands upright or half sits,
red dress always the same, white under-
pants uncovered or hidden   All these
are paintings:  In one Mom lies on the
ground, flung from her yellow throne, arms wide,
her mouth a moan
                              But in the bronze,
*Daddy's Girl*, it's very hard to tell
if either wears clothes   Dazed and wide-eyed,
she grabs his thighs   His hands are over-
sized, the right spans her breast to her waist

In later canvases, she comes to
life:  Inside a tub they sit; he's clothed;
she's not   Now with her legs apart, hands
circle her father's throat, reach from be-
hind   They pull him up—half doll, half corpse—
out of chill water   He wears pinstripes
(black and white), she a red smile

## With Poppies

A girl, one girl, quite blond, her hairbow white,
in nothing but golden shorts, standing straight
as the woman below (*the one she used to be*)
but with differences: head cocked to the right,
her eyes also, more tender, gleaming now;
her lips darker red than the poppy she holds
toward us, stamens and styles on show

                                Squatting
behind her, where shore meets sky, a benevolent
yellow gorilla—his one eye half-lidded,
the other open wide—watches over her
No need for a wall or glass between them here
More so than the others, whether in paint or
bronze, he appears to be kind and slow

A girl? A woman holding a single deep
scarlet upright cup, *Papaver rhoeas*, her
right hand raises it by the stem, above
her bosom, below her collarbone   Red spot,
red center, though higher in the frame

                                  She's
naked: forehead, neck, breasts, sex, and thighs
whiter than limbs or flesh-colored rings around
her deepset eyes   The time: long past summer's end
Her hair gray-black   Her gaze: knowing, wary,
alert, askant   The man she stands in front of lies
on his back; arms cushion his head, wrists crossed,
legs parted, one is raised—almost a *Maja* pose
He casts blue shadows   His eyes calm, closed;
thick lips the color of dried blood   He looks
satisfied   Does he lie on a mattress
or a block of ice? How long can she and
the poppy survive the cold?

# Coronation

He went first   She would follow   At first
she was sad, her face said so   He left,
she looked away   He died; she could not
follow him *all* the way—*yet*—she's here,
and she is not   Her mouth widens in
a cry of pain, the D of *Dasein*—
dementia? delight?  In denial
of life itself, life as we know it

What light can these daughters shed?  Against
a background all black and blood-red   Soon
they'll crown their shrieking mother, blue in
the face and arms and legs, like their dad
(already regnant), a cherry-red-
nosed, drunken clown   Neither one has hands
(*Handfallen* in their language means: at
a loss, bewildered, perplexed)   One hand
poised to halt the action, the older
girl gestures the younger: *No, not yet*
*It isn't time*
               Two old folks sit on
hard green boxes within a circle
of squares that float (as if the squares in
a checkerboard magically lifted
off the table)—orange, yellow, white
Dolls now, with seated shadows   Lena's
shadow, on the right, appears as it
never has before: Lying, stretching
out on the table, recalling
images of their parents which
have oppressed the girls before   Kerstin
waits for her sister's signal to
lower the crown, let Mother go

## Operation

*How old, Lena, do we have to be? How many years (since their deaths)*
*have to pass before we can cut off their limbs and watch them scream?*

Cut them off
now her feet
Cut them off
Here's the knife
It's so easy
just like meat
just like carrots
No, chicken thighs
Grab her toes
and I'll slice
Watch them scream
Hear them scream
Don't!
See their mouths
See Dad's teeth
See their arms
without joints
without hands
See Dad's willy
See his boots
See the blood
spilling down
where we've cut
below his
knees   Here goes
Mom's left foot
Do you think
she'll pass out?

They never had
hands to touch

They had us
They made us

We have them now

## In a Bottle

The sea was not a mask. No more was she.

—Wallace Stevens

No milk ever filled this one
I remember her differently
Older or younger?  Arms
flailing? signaling?  No swimming
tube  *Girl in a Bottle*
I've known her all my life
Pasty pink, almost white herself,
blondie enclosed in glass,
surrounded by maroon

*Det drar, det drar*
It draws the life out of her
She's not a ship, not a
fore-and-aft rig, no schooner
From the waist up naked,
head tilted back, fore-
head butting the bottle
glass, eyes tilting upward—

Turquoise and teal and
turbulent ultramarine
hide legs there's no room for
How can there be waves
in a bottle laid flat on its side?
Sleight of hand!  Unseen
legs!  If they're tucked up
under her, might she leap

through the glass?  Fat
chance!  It is thick as, well,

bottle glass   And she assumes—
though her arms shake the
yellow tube and her red-
ribboned plaits fly back in
defiance—a posture, a stance
She stands firm   She is
rooted   Her outcry is huge

She screams, shows her teeth
Her mouth is wide open
The bottle is stoppered,
sucks out all her breath
Moist breath fills the bottle—
spirit floating in space
She's the form she creates
*Det drar   Det drar*

## Standing Meditation

For Lena on her birthday
31 December 2005

There she stands, all three foot six
of her, tall and proud, wrists down,
fingers spread, arms out in the stance
both you and I know as *Chi Shih*,
Beginning   She leans, head tilted,
shifted right, as if hearkening;
her lips a slight smile   Is she
doing *qigong*? From there—still
a beginner with less than one
year of tai chi in *my* body—
I would shift left, turn right, rais-
ing right toe & right hand, com-
mencing *Lan Chiao Wei*, Grasp Sparrow's
Tail, with the move *we* call Carry
the Baby, proceed to Left
Ward-off, Right Ward-off . . . and so on
Proceed, yes   It's simply not
in us to stand still as statues,
no matter how often our
teachers command us—and each
day we get up and—*Practice!*

There she stands, stood to greet me (to my
immense surprise) on my birthday this
past July, before, and here I mean
set some distance from the entrance to
one part of Samling Saltarvet—more
than a gallery, less than a full-
grown museum—in a small town off
a road on the west coast of Sweden

Not at all the unstopped genie
spiraling out of her bottle   Not
the terra cotta you gave me for
my fiftieth, calmly ensconced in
a striped bowl, embracing her *nalle*
This one is big and bronze and substantial
as you or I   Her twin lives inside,
for now, with other girls who grimace,
 jump rope, kneel, converse with cats or fish
or gorillas. . . .
              Lena, only today
did my mind grind to a halt on s*alt-
arvet*, the word:  literally "salt
legacy" (setting *saltarven*, sea
sandwort, aside)   *Arv* is related
to "orphan" etymologically
No one alive can live without salt!
But our girls, our girlhood, our lot?  Lots
we cast without looking back?  Never
shall they be Lot's daughters, nor shall we
abandon them until we make our
way to the underworld   May they keep
their heads—balanced on necks, torsos, trunks,
legs, and feet—smiling heavenward, grounded
Still standing pillars of bronze, columns
of words

## Self-Portraits: Reflections—Letters to Lena

**12 June 2006**

Dear Lena,

You're chilled on Koster, I'm caught in Stockholm's
heat, sitting at Göran's desk, his *skrivbord*,
where you don't paint—while here you did that
on the long table in the next room
He sits behind me in your painting
at a desk like this (the work completed
in 1966):  One drawer toward
the viewer, the desktop black, he
stretches over a typewriter, green—
*Tag och skriv*, named after Ekelöf's
suite, "Write it Down". . . .

I'm at my laptop  We both gaze at
you through open double doors across
two rooms  You with a round hand mirror,
naked, white or whitish, whiter where
tank-top or swimsuit screened your upper
torso  You wear *The* [titular] *Hat*,
brimmed brown but basically black  You look
away from us and at us both at
once  Your left hand holds a brush, your right
the glass, revealing a grimace your
face—attentive, poised—declines to show:
lips parted, tongue rolled down over the
lower one  This brings a faint smile to
mine  Of course I had to ask about
the carcass on the white palette  A
cormorant:  less common in '83
when you painted this . . .

## 16 June 2006

Lena, dear Lena, another mid-
summer approaches

      Between Day and Night—
      is there really any difference?
      Open-eyed, how blind we are
      how visionary, eyes shut, in sleep

(Ekelöf again, toward the end of
*The Tale of Fatumeh*)

Like an Etruscan on the lid
of a carved chest,  I sleep over
your images   Literally
atop two thin mattresses piled
on flat files, unaware of what's
in them   Down past where my feet
end, small girls on small canvases
One sits bolt upright in a gray
basin of blue water, embraced
by a black cat, whose prehensile
tail curls round her left shin for dear
life   Two stand behind a table
preparing to slice? set to feed?
parents laid out on a blanket

Sometimes I talk to fourteen bronze
sisters who, sitting or kneeling
on top of it, keep the TV
in its corner
          If I open
my eyes during standing medi-
tation, I glimpse the faces of

your *tappade flickor* set on
the windowsills, terra–cotta
*girls'* heads you *dropped* before firing
One corner of each mouth turns up,
the other corner down
                I turn
one palm up and the other down,
slowly return to center and
reverse them
          Swiftly the world spins
more swiftly more harshly than be-
fore   I am learning to root   I
am learning to let things go
past me, or to deflect them
                 *Why*
*sleep when the sky is white, is blue?*
I ask you again on the phone
We make our own works, our own days
We plant, we play, we bear, we take
measures  And yes we will fight, but
not to the death  Death will come
entirely on its own


## 17 June 2006

Soon I'll pack, fly home to New York
where you painted up a storm of new
self-portraits this past winter, smiling,
content  With girls on your hands, both hands:
hand–puppets or marionettes dan-
gling from them without strings; only two
have stuck-out tongues  And head-stacks: totem
poles? I see Athena born and born
again out of her own skull, never numb

but often grimacing   All in good
fun   Heaps of you in twos or threes   Mistress
of self-mastery, all tongue in cheek


*Midsommarafton*, **23 June 2006**

Back in Brooklyn Heights, two days past
the actual solstice   What's private,
what's public about us?   To be a
person is to wear a mask   Your heads,
your bronze masks and bronze mirrors—Whose
face did you cast here?   Whose soul?   Are girls
more or less fragile within glass balls?

Substantial, steely, severe, in three older
self-portraits based on van Eycks, you are
fully dressed; only your face is bare
*The Betrothal* gives us the Arnolfinis
with you and Göran, a cat, your tongue out
in the mirror   In *Madonna* your grown
self sits on your own lap   But in *The Mother*,
you sit enthroned, your aged mother—
doll-sized, firmly in your grasp—clings to your
knees   Your right hand wears a ring set with
a black stone   Is the band gold?
                                    Silver,
in reality, you tell me—We know
better than to trust reproductions . . .
Lena, my dear, *you* are the real thing
When I first saw your work, something went
gold inside me, and ever since then
the seeing part of me writes in its glow

Lots of love,
            Rika & SmileyBear

# SELECTED POEMS

In memory of my mother Celia Fogelhut Lesser

(24 February 1916 – 9 January 2007)

# FIRST POEMS: 1972–1974

## The News & The Weather

I rush to the newspapers.  Seeking
something current.  Weeklies, quarterlies
put timeliness in archives, always
smother me with their musts.  I require:
the press in motion, the past kept back,
letterpress, linotype, cuts, relief.
On television, I only grasp
the weather:  the fronts and whorls, offshore
Agnes, stagnant, menacing the land.

How to love you here, in this *city*—
Garment workers strip me with their eyes.
We live too much inside:  In your flat
only the two front rooms have windows.
The sides of the building are blank brick.
The fire escape sags; its iron base
and ladder end eight feet off the ground.
There is no where to walk.  Every
crosslight is yellow—hesitation.

At night the sidewalk mica flashes.
Buses make every other stop.  Trains
avoid bridges.  The Watchtower waits
for someone to heed its words.  Your kiss
inspects each plane of my flesh like an
elevator, emptied, jarring at
every flaw. You give me no words to heed.
I rush to the newspaper.  On page
twenty-seven, column three, I read:

"On Lake Titicaca's floor, thousands
of giant frogs have grown for years.

The team of French savants who've found them
swear by their savoriness, and though they
fear the hides won't tan, Bolivians
should can the Leviathans." I run
downstairs. Whirlwinds of children pogo
up the street. Disengaged stairways wake
me to the sky. And I fly,
                    I fly

## Let's throw it out the window


How ever did we spend an entire evening re-bending that wire sculpture,
        only to toss it eighteen stories down?
Poor contorted dancer, we gave her whiplash, at least.
The air was so coarse, the friction must have melted her.
I heard no splash in the pool.

This morning I threw the oatmeal out the window.
The air was so cold, the spoonfuls froze into tennis balls.
Naturally, you stood downstairs with a racket.
You volleyed them up to me.

A man in a checkered jacket came to the door.
He claimed to have what we needed; he knew our habits.
Used firemen's nets—mottled ones.
I insisted on houndstooth.

All afternoon, I stared at Magritte's enormous comb standing on its bed,
I lit up a Virginia, pretending to be Brecht.
For the first time I really believed: *"Es sind ganz besonders riechende Tiere . . .
Es macht nichts, ich bin es auch."*

It has been raining ever since.
The rain is one enormous damper for your percussive comments.
Have you nothing inviolable to discuss?
Have you no hand to extend?

## Persons of Prognostication

### I

No work bound me. No worth.
No tongue. Though tongue-tied, sang.
Breathed with love's lungs.
Flew, hung, like a bat. Heard.
As if nature were my nature
And at one.
Lost words.

### II

What we cannot imagine:
How we began,
should not matter
does not matter
in this light.

I would close the door.
Intimacy, a foot
unshod, intrudes.
Riders, bareback, naked,
scrape the heart's floor,
draw its powers.

Come back before
to know and to feel
were discrete.
Come back before
each was so poor.

## III

We start from nothing.
The long ancestral halls
emptied of portraiture
hung with blank tapestries.
Frames were collapsible,
statues dispensable.
Now we are lost.

The men backroom
crowing of prosody,
prudence, propriety,
hold up their spelling charts,
dreaming of numes.

But we dyslexic few
can't tell the rats from the arts
can't tell the stars from the tsars.
How does one
pray?

## IV

Sit down at the piano, Poet.
Be seated in your lassitude.
Give us a tune by Bach, a fugue,
no cadenza here, only the cadence,
clear, as composed.
Not here extemporized
Not to be improvised
Neither of time nor of sight
(nor in sight nor in time)
Not unforeseen.  Give us a
sarabande, an allemande.

Give us the written key.
Something with three repeats.
Not as if of your mind,
less of your self.
Give us a tune by Bach,
a *tune* by *Bach*.


**V**


Harpsichord quill in the ear
Lyre in the heart
The fingers are willing
But the strings are taut.

How does one agonize?
How does one praise?
Where are the harmonies?
Where is the dissonance?
Where is our diffidence?
How does one weep?

In the next room
someone with violin
wails a lament.
Poor little gypsy
always at no request
follows from town to town.

One stays intractable
and masterless.

**VI**

A man walks round my head as if to pray,
As if to capture ritual in motion.

He does not speak, he bids.
He does not say which way to turn,
Yet changes his direction.

I cannot stay his feet
I cannot count or tell
his windings or his bows.
His footsteps without print
batter my brain
and so my brain, my heart.

I hear, I neither feel nor see.
But what?  But what?

## VII

It is so quiet here:
Before the onset:
the .heart's dark door          .
desolate
open.
The locks—fast.

What remains in the veins,
What insists in the heart
to start us once, startle us, leads
to this impasse only.

I do not need you—here
I need the door—ajar
And we—parting. Far—
Oceans—between.

## VIII

You will not recall
my eyes
my hair

You will not recall
what I wore
when we met

We know what has happened
because
it is done.

You will not recall
touching me.
I could not feel
your touch.

We don't know
what possessed us:
Between us: mistrust.
Dreams of lust lasting.
Lost loves. Dust.

What we once held:
(How we held each other once—
You alone could not hold me—)
May we hold once more.

Only the parting posture
for a moment resists
this radiance.

## IX

Feast now my ancestors,
my rightful heirs.
Pull down your handkerchiefs,
loose those wild grins.

First course: of bones:
marrowed and marrowless;
Second: of teeth;
Third: of the corneas;
Fourth: underneath,
down the black hollow shaft
where things inverse
are as they—are.

Pass me the muscatel.

What, am I more than chef?
Am I progenitor?
Is this belief?

## X

Is this the way to recall,
given the chance, to rename,
to call another way,
whisper, not cry?

Bring in the bandits,
outlaws and scalawags,
rapscallious blackguard
knaves. The rogues in rouge.

Why rogue? Why reprobate?
Why from the Underworld?
Fill up the room with smoke!
Bring them to me!

## XI

Who is this old man
walking through my head?
His room is empty
My heart, his bed.
The bed is mountainous
He cannot lie down.
Within these mountains
The man is stone.

## XII  Envoy

Come join me now my love; open the door.
                       You have the power.
What you will find: no well, no tower.
                    Just here, *I* stand.

Here you must give away all that you own.
                       How quickly done!
Poor, you have won.  And as a stone
                   stock-still you stand.

Limestone or marble lips, within each hand,
                   measures of sand.
Nothing endures in this hard land
                  where we two stand.

No sound but my voice is heard in this space.
                   Slowly your face
weathers and scales, features erased,
                  crazed, it may stand.

Love, let me, release me, from what I know.
                    For I must go.
I gave you all.  What can I owe?

                  Free, I will stand.

## Your Speech

for Richard Howard


Even when you said, "The problem with that poem is that it is one
      half Rilke,
one half Wallace Stevens, one half Emily Dickinson . . .
And that's just it!   That poem has three halves!"
flashing video blue eyes, refusing to discuss it further; I
attended
your silences.

Even back in '72, when I hated you desperately, yet believed in the
      occasional wisdoms
your numerous dramatic readings did lead up to . . .   Even
when you asked if your apartment was all I had expected, and (thinking
      of Göteborg's hideous Poseidon), I replied
I had no expectations to speak of.   Even
when you mispronounce my given name, then correct *my* Germanisms,
my prepositions who
are always preposterous
in any language, (but how does one translate
*bis an*, that almost being there, that grammatical
embodiment of completion's *Unmöglichkeit*), I remember, I reconstruct,

O Mentor of Form & Diction,

at that unfair vantage point, advantage and disadvantage in one for
      your ephebe,
I recall that you are also human,
guarded, liberal.

## The Room

In the room that's known no fire in seven years
I build one, strike a match; it seems more real
to me in Swedish: *en tändsticka*, a tinder
stick, watch the blue walls behind the cigarette's
blue smoke, uninhaled, and the spent gray (there is
ash gray in these ice blue walls) cast their nets.
On the desk, a still life: teapot and strawberry
cheesecake. Wanting coral ceiling, yellow walls.

The room is always as I left it:
furniture, few possessions, new stacks
of junk mail from the months away. How
did I choose the draperies, the bedspread,
with their kellies, turquoises, umbers on
white? What flowers were ever like these?
On the dresser, a bowl of fresh-cut,
maroon chrysanthemums is glaring.
November. Outside the white window
maple leaves still cling. In Brooklyn, things
hold on longer.

I remember the night the room flared from
the orange carpet to one of the beds
with its yellow sheet: a cheesecake iced
with flaming clothes! Leaving my own white room
for the smoke-filled hall that smelled like dinner
(how we mistake the actual for the known),
I called to my heedless sister in the guest room,
"Fran, get off the phone; your room's on fire!"
Tumbling downstairs. Outside the lightly
falling snow. February. The blue room
is always February.

We kept our lives and, for the first days, strength.
Only two ceilings crumbled from the rot
of heavy water. The eyes of the house, upstairs,
knocked out, boarded up. Fran and I slept
downstairs, in the living room. In the basement
our parents. What floor-sweeping demons there were
entered my mother. She came from herself.
What Lares and Penates lurked, abandoned
her. Perhaps the scrolls in the mezuzas burned.
The eyes of the house, knocked out, boarded up.
Each day she wept, as if blind with cataract.

We were under-insured, that is, too
self-assured, but came out all right, got
to buy new clothes, clean of smoke, and went
on going to school, were precocious,
bratty. Fran said I sat up in my sleep
speaking of certain plants sopranos
ate. We talked; we shared no secret
language. "Braint plants . . ." *Burnt* ones? *Brained?*

The months went by. Depressions, doctors, drugs,
shock treatment, love. (How is it that a house
takes hold of you? Why do I dream of theaters,
opera houses? Who are these stunned and gaping
elderly people?) *Hon var ifrån sig*, she came
from herself. Got "well."
                                    I think, when I'm
home for a visit, she opens the door
to my room to see if her memory
of me holds on. She keeps the house. Protects
each room. Or do they own her?

Phantastes, Eumnestes, Nameless One who holds
the Present. I must be Anamnestes who

calls to mind again, retrieves. She is Alma.
For a time, she is with us again. This Thanks-
giving. Now I leave, don't like to travel, though
I need to be in new places. In each room
I set books and yellow roses. I try to
keep my house within my head. It is enough
that the heart operates the rest of the body.
I recall only blueprints, monuments,
architectural dreams.

# Ein Geliebtes:  The Body of the Work

for R. M. R.

## I.  Approach

Because you were not mine, I approached
you as I would any human being:  hesitantly,
close-mouthed, from a distance. You seemed
both alive and dead, and I tried to work you
out from what others said about you.
Others who thought they knew you.
If I think back to our first meeting, our first
encounter, what impressed me most was your way
of walking:  precise in every step.
There are, after all, walls between us.
And a background:  but I too can see, "a round shard
with a red ground, upon which the taut legs
of a quadriga appear, like the black inscription
over an entrance."

So I returned your call, though at first
you were belligerent, even openly hostile to me:
Taunting me with puns, inventing words, or worse—
altering the old ones, with no respect for grammar.
Not trusting hearsay, I came to you myself
and held on tight until your Protean forms:
dead body of Christ, horses, butterflies,
eyelids of black-eyed roses, clear lachrymatories,
fruits, mirrors, angels, gods and God knows what
turned and returned to one thing with no name,
something nameless and unspeakable. Like a magician
of the invisible, a clock without hands, you pointed to
things in you, in me, somewhere between:  Images.
My curse on the words!

## II. Depths

Like Christ's soul in Hell I plunged wilder
depths, heard cries howl toward me.
When the landscapes vanish, is it
my voice that speaks?  Late at night,
in one ruinous flash, like an exhibitionist
you'll say, "I am your sleeper," and disappear.
Then like a painter faced with blanks, knowing
only no color is absolute, I reconstruct
from tone.  Kinder than most, you utter
no loud demands, never look hurt, revenge
is not in your nature.  But you just stand there,
clear as the Design in a cloudless sky at night,
and just as constant.

You've made your own defense, down to each
dash that punctuates a pause—, where
I hear music, see a rush of rain, feel a power
descending.  But not to me; perhaps to me alone.
You delivered me from my chores to my work,
my real address.  Some have too little faith.
We approximate in choosing.  But are we lost?
We can only lose ourselves.  And one good man
encouraged me to sustain our difficult rapport,
one flamboyant man
with the courage of all the French nation.

## III. Vows

There are times I think our affair will never work out.
Bonds delude.  Ceremonial diction rings false in
my voice.  Praise cannot.  Fruits rot, fall away:
but sometimes decay brings forth.  The tree rises,
green ascends.  How often have I had to turn to Root.

So dark down here, if I look up for an instant,
I'm sure to lose you.  I must look down
far down within myself, until I become
transparent, and your print, your imprint emerges.
No one can part us.  Few can give advice.
You are my crutch as long as I make you walk.
If there's a god in me, may it be the one of song.
May our words be flung into the invisible and there
live.  If I turn wayward or willful,
give me your elegies.

# Rika Lesser

for Paul Zelinsky

## I. Cantus Firmus

In your painting of me, Paul (it has
no name), why have you split me at night
with a mirror? After three sittings
and some twenty stills you whited out
the 4 x 7 foot canvas, turned
it to make me stiller, stiffer than
the taut surface you covered. What you
uncovered was more than you could guess.

## II. Descant

Each is a poet, outside and in. The one in the room
knows duty: to be charming in conversation,
to express the unutterable only in print.
Her pose or gesture is relaxed but closed:
One hand fingers a paper on her anatomically
impossible and larger-than-life lap, the other
clamps it there. The head tilts back and up. The eyes
are off somewhere, lackluster, as if to track
the land or seascape she has never made. The heart's
not there, the lips won't form a kiss, and the heart
of the matter: not compassion, but composure,
a surmise of bearing. That newspaper on her lap
should have been Dickinson, or at least a dictionary.
Betrayal. An earlier sketch reveals the head of
Rilke above a hanging plant. But finally,
there are only two, who should be one. Here it is true.

But the portrayal of that other, darker
self in the sea! Larger than the cliffs at her
feet, and the collapsing derrick in the distance.
That drawn-out reflection in the glassy Night,
not the stretched freak on a spoon, but the globes
of a chandelier on the tea's surface, far
down in the cup. That one—a poseuse deft
in her practice—someone to face. Someone whose
averted face the girl in the room knows
but won't recognize. The lights that fall
on this canvas are all false. Evening breaks
promises, promises of embracing all
we have no right to—the Dead we cannot possess,
the dead in ourselves. Better to see by night
when images sink in, when no embrace exists—
only the lights in mirrors, the points of light.


### III. Incantation

The girl in the seascape, whose lips won't move, would say:
    *If you claim nothing of me, I will not hold you to your words.*
    *Claim nothing of me, for I build a city within.*
    *Do not try to move me, the sea is my root.*
    *Do not try to hold me, the sky is my hold.*
    *Offer no shelter, my breath fills the space*
    *between stars. By my own lights I read.*
    *I see as I see by them. My houses are blazing:*
        *Closed To All But Night.*

## IV. Canticle

Give me your words, Night, to place above the doors,
the proper names, not the ones used in there
where the red-cheeked girl serves tea and reads by
artificial light.  No more than a statue
can sing can I say those two into one.

Give me my name, syllables I can bear
and pronounce at sunrise.

# BLUEPRINTS AND MONUMENTS: 1974-1983

# The Gifts

## I

The first box is as long as your arms
and round, a hatbox to take to heart
not head.  Inside: a drum, tympanum
that beats by itself for you. When you
run, it works your lungs, and sounds as if
small, well-formed feet danced on its rim.
Place it under your bed; it helps you sleep.
Not manufactured.  Comes in one size.
Involuntary and invaluable.


## II

If you can unbind all the bands—
for it seems this is a ball of
nothing but them—you may then un-
ravel this sphere of wigs:  some long
and loose, some braided and done up,
toward the center, short and shingled.
A disguise for each discomfort.
The core, irrevocably, is
a mirror with no frame or stand,
just a hook at the top.  For women only.

III

A single railroad car, on weekends
computerized to run between
Tashkent and Raivola. On weekdays
the decor ranges from watered-silk
chaise longues to velvet davenports.
Entrance: Grand Central, go down several
flights to Lexicon Parvenu Line.
Poets half-rate on round trips at all times.


IV

A set of dictionaries:  Swedish-Danish
                        Danish-Portuguese
                        Portuguese-Persian
                        Persian-Armenian
                        Armenian-Sanskrit
                        Sanskrit-Chinese
                        Chinese-English.
All volumes but the first are in preparation
and will be sent by sea, one every three years.

## V

Countless tapes, poised and point–device,
educational matter, non-
erasable: commentaries
on your work by experts speaking
nothing but their own limita-
tions. Pamphlet enclosed—transcripts in
French and German. Play at half-speed.
These voices against your own.

## VI

Acme Lego Kit: links that form nothing but
stairways (imitation marble)—Only for
Ascent. And on the landing, columns (Doric).
Miniature wind-up puppets optional.
If they back up, or pause for cigarettes, down
they wind until what life you granted trips them
up. They fall to the threshold. The structure burns
or folds. Supply is limited. See listings
in Section Six under Origami Homes.

# Departures

In memory of Moris Fogelhut (1879-1970)


**I.** *Ich habe Tote, . . .*


The broken chair of wood, mahogany—the one that used
to be his, with cushions of fluffy gold brocade, changed
by his daughter, later, for something flatter, more
American in pattern, almost colonial, even as he lived
with us in the house; the small oak table with liberty
bells cut out of its sides, two shelves for books or whatnots;
the paired twin beds with bells in bas-relief on the headboards,
missing, burned long ago in another room;
the four-poster he died in, naturally, now mine:
these furnishings rebuke my heedlessness: as if I sinned
the day he died—not practicing piano in the morning
before I left. Reproach me—for not having wept enough,
for not learning the siddur, the mahzor, the Torah—
for keeping appointments, customs, never faith.

Because we name our children for the dead, I am "Rika,"
after his only wife. In our albums she is sturdy and
large-breasted, almost stern. The name, as given to me,
had no meaning. Passed down like a poem conned to rote.
And yet we learn it does mean "limb" in Bulgarian,
"pear blossom" in Japanese, "rich" in Swedish; often
misspelled, and either mispronounced at birth or ever since . . .
What is mine by custom is empty of meaning.
Only a word that I must renew. What was I born to:
Galicia, his *glil-ha-goyim*, turned in for a new land,
when and why forgotten. Short-sighted, my grandfather
might fail to recognize me in the street. But how he'd keep
the Sabbath, how his hands would hold the keys to the temple.
How he would touch the doorposts when he entered or left.

**II.** *. . . und ich liess . . .*

Why do you live in Sweden?

> *Because my work is portable.*

Why?

> *Because I had a lot to leave.*

What do you speak?

> *Swedish, English, sometimes German.*

What?

> *I have not said one word in three months.*

Do you feel safe?

> *Ja visst!*

Do you?

> *Only in the dark.*

How do you spend your evenings?

> *Writing, writing many letters, many words.*

How?

> *I sleep with a strange man every night.*

In your letters you wrote you had many friends.

> *In my letters I am given to lies.*

In your letters . . .

> *Yes I had friends; all are dead to me.*

Would you prefer that we did not come to see you?

> *Stay where you are lest you see me as I am.*

Would you prefer . . .

> *Of course you must come, you are all I have left.*

**III.** . . . *sie hin*

Leaving, yes. When I returned that day, he was still warm
with death. He had just asked once more for the plain box of pine.
Never having known me as now I am: thinner, full
of languages he had no use for.
He is the old man walking through my head,
a memory scratching like a cane on slate.
Whose was that slogan, *Death will set me free?* Renew,
rejuvenate—words that must expire. If I render them
I do not give them up. These are my words, my landscape,
the peoples I am heir to. All that we have
is not all we possess. We can give twice as much—
like the mirror that upsets us in the morning
consoling us at night. What was it Rilke wrote?

> *We have, where we love, only this:*
> *to release each other, for to hold one another*
> *comes easily to us, and need not be learned.*

To release each other, to widen the freedom
in our poverty we name "love," by giving back,
by returning to what has been freely given.

## Growing Back

for Judith Hoberman


The overgrown plant, billed as a cactus, but surely
a sedum of sorts: parts of it properly upright,
others, stems, half dead, with persistent tips, clusters
of fleshy leaves trailing the withered pink blooms, effortless,
sessile, removed to a table, since spring will not come
though it's April 14th, the window-ledge battered
by corn-snow, the jambs dropping melted sleet. The plant I bought
only one of this year, knowing it would be just
one year I might keep it. It could do with a larger pot
and doubtless will when I give it away. It will be
time to give up every thing again; but now I cling
to these surroundings, can scarcely raise myself from bed
regardless of sleep or time.


In a dream I lent out my lexicons, even
the *O.E.D.* and *Webster's Third New International*,
abandoning these for a diction. Some other voice
than Reason's dictated this. Some other dictator
indited, commanding me leave my stays and enter
a world of forms, spaces, chambers enclosed but roofless,
sands over my head, the sea distant but present.
I never speak in my dreams though I talk in my sleep.
I have never woken screaming. Stifling I've tried
to scream and woken; no incubus perched on my sternum.
Voices I have heard: a word or two spoken sagely,
distinctly, irrevocably; or sounds, birds or bells.
I myself have never answered.


In a dream I removed a particolored blouse
and with it all the color of my bruised arms.
Another: I walked out among rocks, sands and seabrush;

each one spun on its own axis. Wrapped in a caftan,
I tried to reach firm ground, touched something
and covered my face with my hands. When I took them off
they were caked with blood and my face completely charred.
This too came off, a black thickness with the mouthprint
still clinging. In another room, girls screamed, women
drew blood from a man's chest, the police were coming . . .
I could not leave that house.

I have been walking in my sleep again. Where I've been
no one knows, but my footsoles smart as if parched
by hot sands. I woke to raining slush, chilled through,
though my feet were burning. I woke and rose only
because something rang, and the ringing disrupted
my hand furiously writing away on the sheet.
What I wrote no one knows. It was a letter
with letters sloping uphill.

Has it been long since I wrote? I can't keep track, had counted
on you as clock and calendar. You kept track for me.
I have been down in the caked sand at the shore between tides.
Not as the rootless sea palm with its crown of blades,
but as the lug, *Arenicola*, casting a mound of my form
behind, above me. Found nothing. Turned back.—
Out of context, many things can be bridged, nothing changed.
And the bridges we think we have burned behind
are more secure than any destination.

Write me again of your wedding, the glow that lit
everyone that day; or of married life, tender
distractions, backgrounds submerged. I want to invent
a new dance, a new ritual, with my own tempo,
somewhat out of time. There will be no music,
just the sequence of words: I begin I begin I begin.
And the dance is a ring, but no hands are joined,

just extended, palms half up, fingers curled inward,
one hand before the other . . .

It grows all too clear, what I set out to do without
ambition and beyond reward. I have taken too many
into my keeping, careful to possess none.
To keep my balance: this distance. I am exhausted
not fatigued. When I pass a mirror I haven't the strength
to look. I am still tempted to believe the heart
does nothing but pump blood, the hand touches nothing
it does not disturb. I want to walk weary, naked
in the night, under clear stars, on a path unfolding
with each step. Nothing more than the mind of the sedum
breathing through its limbs, of the tumbleweed, before autumn.

## Værøy

> The island in the distance . . . is called by the Norwegians Vurrgh. The one midway is Moskoe. . . . These are the true names of the places— but why it has been thought necessary to name them at all is more than either you or I can understand. . . .
>
> —E. A. Poe, *A Descent into the Maelström*


The last outpost is on its eastern coast, facing Mosken.
The cries of ravens veer off the telephone poles
which trail off to Mostad, an abandoned fishing village.
A narrow footpath chases the mountain ridges.
Winding along it, you will catch and lose sight of Mosken:
an enormous supine parrot, the sun caught in its beak.
The path is six inches wide and covered with sheep-droppings.
On the left, a wall of mossy crags; on the right, a steep drop.
(Sometimes the sheep stumble on the rocks and slide:
tiny white avalanches to the sea.)
The trail winds down to water. The beach is underwater.
You walk on sea-smoothed rocks, watching for dry ones.
Among them, pools of decomposing seaweed,
rust-orange pools of rotting sea palms.
Green sponges fringe the undersides of boulders.
A six-toed puffin hound digs for off-white eggs.
At last a marker: Kalkluovnen, the bird-rocks
sculptured and gray, the quicklime furnace.

Within the folds and gorges of Kalkluovnen
the black-backed gulls and razorbill auks all stand
with their beaks toward Greenland
in rows of silhouettes, no two the same.
Rainbow-billed puffins (Norwegians call them "sea-parrots")
like flying sausages dive for stippled sea urchins,
while the querulous kittiwakes bicker and screech

shooting off clusters and tufts of feathers.
The North Atlantic eats at a cliff
which becomes a male profile, thirty meters high.
He is "Tussen," a huge troll, and stares over the ocean.
Far above, white-tailed sea eagles float and pass out of sight.

Back at the marker, a road opens to Mostad.
Remnants of iron railings guide you; the ground is solid.
The island narrows, you cross back to its east coast.
The interior, westward, is bird-punctured stone.
Across the bay is a white strip of beach called Sanden,
rising from it, a black tabula rasa, one thousand feet high.

Poe saw nothing of this, "giddy, atop Helseggen,"
the knife-edged peak of the goddess whose face is half human
half blank.  In the province of Nordland, sunlit all summer,
sixty-eight degrees north, beyond the Maelström is Værøy:
Nesting Place, Island of Rams, Weather and Wind.
All this it gives you. Værøy, not Vurrgh, is the given name.

## Translation

Lost: the Original, its Reason and its Rhyme,
Words whose meanings do not change through time,
"The soul in paraphrase," the heart in prose,
Strictures or structures, meter, *les mots justes*;
"The owlet umlaut" when the text was German,
Two hours of sleep each night, hapax legomenon,
A sense of self, fidelity, one's honor,
Authorized versions from a living donor.

Found in translation: someone else's voice:
Ringing and lucid, whispered, distant, true,
That in its rising accents falls to you,
*Wahlverwandtschaft*, a fortunate choice,
A call to answer, momentary grace,
Unbidden, yours; a way to offer praise.

# Losses

for Gunnar Ekelöf (1907-1968)

## I. A Photograph

Before you on the table, a room you wanted
to describe. One of those bronzed decors with cut-glass
chandelier, low paneling, a restless Turkish rug.
It is *vårvinter*, spring in the power of winter.
Furniture: gilded, late-Gustavian,
embroidered, pinstriped, stuffed. A wooden tabletop
rests on bent-legged 8's cut off at the bottom and top.
Past the portraits and sagas turned copperplates,
past the one of Odysseus—the piano clenches
its teeth at the windows. The light hesitates.
Even the photograph turns its back on the windows.

Inside, your father, one more silent witness,
plunged in a rococo fauteuil,
perched on a pile of comforters,
in morning jacket, stiff. Someone has wedged
a white napkin between his collar and chin.
The forehead high, the eyebrows prominent,
the nose short and straight, the chin strong.
The eyes look out at the photographer,
who is not there, as if to follow
what he does or did, but they are lost
in thought, subhuman, fragmentary. Inside
his cool forehead, a swarming coral reef.
Thoughts not inhuman, only "horrible."
Horror is meaninglessness.

## II. Near the Church of John

In a cold land you were born
and your family moved, during the first
world war, from hotel to hotel, settled
awhile in Stockholm, by the Church of John.
You went home to that room and found him
surrounded by nurses, cheerfully
calling you, "Grandpa, little Grandpa!"
At sundown you stood while the brick-red church
threw its red reflection even into
the darkest corner. And the churchbells rang.
And you stood there questioning.

Having stained the costly light-red Milanese
brocade on one of the chairs a litmus blue,
Having been allowed "to sit with the others
at the table," though the yolk spilled over his chin,
Having brooded, without words, in rising tones
incomprehensible strings . . .
Having used you as an oracle for his Psalter,
Having been troubled, humored, lucid, insane, unloved—
Gerhard Ekelöf died of syphilis.

## III. Imago

No more than we can forget the fathers
who were not there
can we forgive the mothers who were
but gave no warmth.
On the bed with bronze paws
the same dream returns and returns.
Sleepless we wrap those shreds of blankets
from a city of ruins around us.

Panayía, Holy Virgin, Virgin of Night
how were we born?
*To want, some are born to want.*
Átokos, Mother of All, of No One,
what will we come to?
*Your mother and your father*
*Yours only by chance.*
Fatumeh, weaning your child,
what must we do?
*He who does not hope knows no despair:*
*Dream the mother you never had.*
*He who does not doubt believes nothing:*
*Know the father you never had.*
*Believe nothing. You will find your name.*

## Under the Roof

I am not sleeping and again the sun
is rising.  Even the Wandering Jew
raises its arms, as if singing.
"Attack the enemy!" *The Outer Limits*
blares from the screen.  An attack
of nerves, or is it habituation?
Sleeplessness—Sweden in winter—
when nights were clearer than days.
Last winter I moved into a building
in Brooklyn Heights, beside
the Lutheran's lone bell, opposite
the Presbyterian's off-key carillon.
The space was calm.
The building had stood a long time.
Across the street the brownstones
are painted numerous shades of red.

I came with a piano and the best
intentions.  I came for the high
ceilings, the loft bed, the gas stove,
for the alcove, the recessed windows,
the archways, but hear footsteps
on the ceiling, voices in the bath,
eternities from one day to the next.

An alarm goes off.  A voice asks:
—Do you know eternity?
—Do you know eternity?
—Do you know what time it is?
Below my windows they are speaking loud
and their accents are surprising on a Sunday
here in Brooklyn.  At the tops of their lungs

German is what they are speaking, waking all
would-be late-sleepers within stone's throw
of the Deutsche-Evangelisch-Luther-Zions Kirche.
Half the church says '39, the other '87,
and the signboard (*Herzlich willkommen*)
reads: Founded in 1855. The bell tolls.
—It must be 11 A.M.

The building has stood a long time.
Through the floors I feel the Hotel
Saint George battle the 7th Avenue Dragon.

## 527 Cathedral Parkway

Squatting under the weight
of the balcony they support,
four gargoyles in need of cleaning:

The first, hunched over a bowl,
raises a spoon to his gaping mouth—
the Black Hole of Cathedral Parkway.
His right foot has four toes
with lots of dirt between them.
His nose is long, blunt at the tip.
He must be very hungry—lids
lowered, eyes only for his food.

The second is bald, bends
over a book, his filthy beard
caught among the pages. One
eyebrow raised, both eyes dart
to the left; they have a knowing look.
In his right hand a heavy plume.
If he's an artist, the arts are black.

The third, alchemist or cook,
clutches a cauldron. Flames lick
its bottom. He looks younger
than the others, lacks a tooth,
sticks out his tongue, touches
it with a finger.

The fourth, greedy, *very* greedy,
has a whole roast chicken on a platter.
He is not intent on eating, only
on keeping it for himself. His legs

bend in the lotus position; in every
other way he's a dog.

Eastward, their four twin brothers hold up
another balcony, but in a different order:
*The Cook, Jack Sprat, Rover, The Leery Sage.*
Higher up, over us all,
ten heads as well as two gryphons
drop their blessings on all who pass.

## 536 Saratoga Avenue

Driving by it now—walking in Brownsville
is no longer safe—536 remains
the only semi-private house on the block.
Everything else has changed: The tenements
across the street are gone. Nothing
replaces them. On our side, burnt and
blown-out frames surround empty courtyards.

Long before I was born, my mother's family
bought the house. Grandmother Ruchtcha died.
I bear the English name she took at
Immigration. Had she not died, I would be
someone else—a name is powerful.

Sharing a bedroom with my middle sister,
I wondered why the playroom was not my own.
Too young to remember Grandfather's moving
out. He lived nearby, across a busy street,
then in the downstairs flat, then in a "home."
Finally, he lived with us; the playroom his again.

My eldest sister had the long front room.
In the street you knew when she talked
on the telephone: she'd stick her feet
out the jalousie windows. Now a wide
strip of tape masks a bifurcation.

Of course, there were other rooms, other doors,
but one of those farthest back completes the tour.

The full bath was called "Rika's bathroom"
because I hogged it. In my sleep I'd walk there.

Awake I'd drown my toys, imagining the room
to be an island.  Shipwrecked, I allowed myself
a large box of cream-filled cookies.  With water,
soft towels, the clothing in the hamper,
I'd do all right.  I won't allow myself to imagine
what goes on there now.  What the small black boy,
who rode a tricycle when we drove past
last summer, would think if he found
scratched with the head of safety-pin
on the tile wall beneath the towel rod
my name.

*1977*

## Menorah

Through tears she inspected all their lives
had been, as if they were dead together.
Nothing could wash them from her mind; they
burned like acid eating through copper.

Fluid yet fixed, trembling branches of a tall
spruce thrashing in crosswinds. A single tree
strung in the darkness with strange lights:
white, blue, and amber.

Caught in the wind their arms traced
circles: hands in prayer over lit candles.
Like her mother veiled with the sacred cloth,
she lit candles. Watched the tree burn.

## Under the Weather

The sky is lead and all our
disappointments fall from it
like pears heavy in autumn.
The radiator drips from
its turn-on valve, needs to be
bled.  Outside, on the sill, scabs
of exfoliated paint
disintegrate to powder.
Across the street, in a top
floor apartment, a shirtless
man opens a window, waits,
extends his arm, leaves my line
of sight. Two floors below, green
plants inhabit the windows,
screen the movements of tenants
whose bedroom walls are patterned:
blue and white vertical stripes.

*A Lesson in Up and Down*
the painting above my desk,
is lit like the sky:  Gray light
on a blue mirror gives back
a lamp's inverse reflection,
a half-open swinging door
leading into the darkest
of rooms, the L of molding
where the walls meet the ceiling.
On the circular mirror,
pastels clustered like pick-up
sticks (red, yellow, and green) float,
the lifter, orange, apart
from the group. A pair of sun-

glasses are iridescent,
their superficial eyes cool
images of the pear-shaped
incandescent bulb, lunar
phases eclipsed by the lamp-
shade's rim. The lamp itself? We
see only its base, large in
the upper left corner of
the canvas, invisible
in the mirror that rests on
a table spread with shiny
violet cloth.
We can only assume that
the painting is true. The real
lamp joins its base, the bulb
will need replacing. On some
other day the glasses shield
actual eyes, the table
laid with plates and food that won't
keep. Today the sky threatens
to eat our breath, presses down,
compresses us to surface,
makes our flesh pigments
in a still life.

## Eight Days a Week

### Monday through Thursday

What I began to hear on Monday night
I firmly believed was: the faucet dripping,
leaves dropping off the plants,
objects falling in a closet on the other side of the wall,
the creaking hinges of the bathroom door when air blew through the vent. . . .

But Tuesday morning I learned what those
noises meant. The poisoned food in a dish
(set under the fridge by an exterminator
months before) splattered out on the kitchen
floor a random mosaic of grains. Next,
the conventional trap:
people tell you
the best baits are chocolate, raisins,
peanut butter, bread. . . .    Helped by a friend
who kills rattlers with a .38,
I move the icebox, vacuum the scattered
food, bait the trap with raisins, set it
out in clear view.

After a restless night (every footstep on
Henry Street is potential mouse-movement),
I talk myself down from the loft bed, make
a phonecall and the mouse appears:
small, gray, adorable, scarcely two
inches long. Into the phone I scream:
"IT SAW IT!" meaning the mouse the food.
The mouse darts out again. I do not see
where it goes.
        Topo Gigio, Mighty Mouse,
Ignatz, women on tabletops and

easy chairs hoisting their skirt hems . . .
What can the creature do? I am 200
times its size, at least—and spend
the night away.

Home with "a better mousetrap" on Wednesday:
a cage with a spring door, gnawproof, made in
Brazil. If you buy several you can start
a menagerie, tease your cat. Still, the tins
of d-CON, the boxes of Mouse Pells and
TAT inform you that mice may fast for two days
before wolfing the feast you prepare, eat
only in private, don't like bright lights, loud
sounds. How many days can I play old Beatles
albums at top volume? Roaches rise
in my esteem. . . . If the trap works
should I give the creature the run
of Brooklyn Heights?
Should I place it, cage and all, on
my landlord's desk?

Friday through Monday

At first my Mouse Motel was a failure:
Friday the Thirteenth found it aslant,
unentered; the mouse had scooted by.
A friend and I discover a stash
of grain under the stove. He cleans there,
I remove a stack of old Sunday
Times sections from the fireplace—only
to find another hoard in one corner.
The mice of my father's childhood
raided the bathroom, shredding toilet
paper to line their nests. With sweaty
palms I lift a batch of outsize envelopes
off the floor beside my desk, feel and

see a shivering ball of fur jump off them.
I screamed. It ran. I found myself
standing on a chair.

Deathtrap baited and snug by the mouse's
lair, I leave again. Saturday morning's
phonecall is obituary. Later
I learn the rodent my friend disposed of
was three inches long. Could it have grown
so fast on a diet of poisoned food?

Sunday I flood the kitchen with
ammonia, blast *Die Fledermaus* all
afternoon. That night, in a hypnagogic
state, did I hear small feet pad across
the living room floor? A few deep
breaths. Morning came, mercifully.

Not expecting results, I bait the Motel
with cheese, catch myself wishing I had
a full-time job. At three I return to
an eerie stillness. I glance at the trap,
glimpse a caged mouse, two inches long,
its longer tail, motionless, stuck in
the metal door. My right hand grabs the neck
of a bottle of scotch, my left the phone.

The *Mousquetaire* enters, dons rubber
gloves, with a bent-wire sword fishes the trap
out from under the stove. *"Mais c'est un bébé!"*
he cries while I fill the kitchen sink
with boiling water. We agree that killing
live creatures is worse than bagging the dead.
I buy new deathtraps, clean, bait, conceal.
Tomorrow may tell. The night's been quiet
so far

## CAN ZONE or THE GOOD FOOD GUIDE

What do you mean, you "don't like poetry"?
Did someone force you, as a child, to taste
rancid stanzas, tainted, reeking lines, so poetry
made you sick (not at heart but) to your stomach?  Poetry
laid on thick, like peanut butter, may take
its time dissolving on your palate.  Poetry
thin as gruel's unpalatable.  Still, poetry
made well, like a fine soufflé, will rise and stand.
How can I make a herbivore understand
that words are flesh *and* grass in poetry,
fish and fowl, birdflight, signs we read,
transforming themselves and us because we read?

Twelve years ago in the Tribune I happened to read
about GIANT BOLIVIAN FROGS.  Of them I made poetry.
Frenchmen canned them, leaving enough to breed,
while chefs the world over steamed, roasted, grilled, and decreed:
No other known creature has such an unusual taste
or transmutable texture.  And then the rumors spread:
*BIG FROGS RADIOACTIVE! THE DEVIL'S OWN EGGS!*
        *DRED-*
*GE LAKE TITICACA!*  The strangest tales take
shape in poetry.  Put down your *Times* and take
less heed of current events.  In Ovid you'll read
how the will to change could help a girl withstand
indecent advances.  See, by the pond, that stand

of laurels—"*Croak!*" blurts a frog.  "Old myths don't stand
a chance in the—*blouagh*—modern world!  Let's read
of true metamorphoses.  Once we had to stand
in for a human prince; but our royal stand-
ard bore a crowned frog salient, King of Poetry!

Marianne Moore, who showed a firm understand-
ing of the natural order, took the witness stand
in behalf of our cousins (she had discerning taste):
In 'imaginary gardens' (not really to our taste)
place 'real toads'; they, warts and all, set stand-
ards for poetry. Subjects, be literal, take
us at our word. Nothing can be worth tak-

ing that serves but once. Amphibians always take
new leases on life; we are its double stand-
ard. Snakes shed their skins, but only we will take
ours off and eat them. Survive! Make no mistake,
on land, in water, you've got to learn to read
between the lines. Don't eat my words, take
them to heart: Leaps, turns, liberties, take
them all; change and be changed or poetry
will die!" Double-talk? Free speech? What else but poetry
encompasses so much? What else can take
bitter experience and camouflage its taste
so we may feed and live and breathe and taste

the next sunrise? What other art can make us taste
what we see: the golden egg whose rising we take
for granted, or set our sights on goose (tast-
ier still) all at once, prodding our taste
buds (smell those cracklings!), forcing our senses to stand
up and take notice? What else awakens taste
for the fruits of knowledge or plants an aftertaste
of first things in apples bitten and apples read?
What but this art can keep our daily bread
from going stale in our mouths?
                                    "To each his taste,"
you say; "I'm hungry and all this talk of poetry
won't fill my gut!" —That only proves poetry

's power of suggestion. "But what if poetry
still gives me indigestion?" —A little taste
will surely settle the question. "What do you take
me for, a guinea pig?" —A hungry child who can't stand
being fed. The world's your oyster. Open wide, now. Read.

# ALL WE NEED, AND MORE: 1986–1992

## BLACK STONES I

It is Thursday, raining
You ask me a question   I
try to answer quickly
definitively or thought–
fully for truly I
do not know
                        I go off to
think—but nothing answers—
so hard so long I lose sight

And you who asked are no
longer there   Or you are—though
not as the person who
asked the question   Only as
a mask or a mirror
someone some thing without Life

Answer me, Death Mask, I
have a question!
                        Through the holes:
feeble breathing, a faint
gleam where the eyes go   Silence

                        And the masks of those I loved
                        answer solely from their love
                        which seeks to heal, but kills

## BLACK STONES IV

You look at me
with waste in your eyes
eyes laid waste
                    I see
lines
retreating—in haste or
slow, definite
                    files

        (isolate, inviolate, we
            need not imagine these wars)


Do not go!  This
is not the same
ground, the same
battlefield
            On whose
have you lost?  In whose
eyes?

        We share
        no history—only
        this moment
        when feeling
                    streams
        through the eye


130

# BLACK STONES VI

## (Falling)

We're strange (some of us)    Not
having been loved enough
demonstrably enough
we are shaken, don't know
what to make of your
*Liebeserklärungen*
loving phrases uttered
years too late (for whom?)

Since my break my father
states, iterates:  *I
love you, I always have!*
supports me now in
every way he can
So that something of
compassion (*Mitleid*
really) can rise in me
But love—the kind one
heedlessly falls
into—the art of
falling itself?

Calling drunk in the dead
of night, to tell me
three years ago you "fell,
fought not to fall madly,"
your passion for me (as
you see me) was not so
much shocking as crude
I told you the truth—

albeit slant: When we
met I instantly liked
you, was pained to learn
you were not unattached

Old Friend, Would-be
Paramour, you set me
on a shaky pedestal,
leave all your burden
in my hands then tie them
behind my back
                    Perhaps
my thoughts are too grave and
what was said has slipped
your mind, "stoned" as you were,
as you like to call it—
But now, hands bound, heavy
of heart, weighted, I am
falling (unable to
reach out or grasp)   Don't know
into what or from where
Only that you are not
with me   And this is not
the first time

## Matthew's Passion

Easter Sunday.  Matthäus Passion spins.
(Have been revising "A Valediction,"
avoiding writing this.)  Can't seem to get
past the first disc's aria, *Buß' und Reu'*.

Yesterday we dyed eggs (it was my
first time). We all laughed while I reddened,
blowing; out oozed the mess. Then you were
too drained for St. Mary's smoky Mass.
The tubes taped to your chest—attached to
a Walkmanlike thing—had kept you from
sleeping; now they deprived your trusting,
greedy eyes of the spectacle: fire
and water and darkness and light, and
Resurrection.  I don't know a soul
who burns with life like you.  A long list
of "last things" remains for you to do.

Six weeks back you felt fine, felt as well
a twinge of remorse, discussing friends
who share your illness, reveal your fate.
The risk's too great:  you can't visit them.
Last weekend you spoke of suicide:
pills you intend to take "when the time
comes." You will need help.  I clammed up.
Out of sympathy and in conflict.

The time hasn't come, thank the Lord, we
can go on indulging in horror
films, pick translations apart, bitch when
the mercury shoots above sixty
degrees, diagnose those who shun all

talk of your dying as if Death were
the disease . . .

If only getting down onto my knees
or if writing could work a miracle,
I would not make you well—immortal!
I miss you even now. After we use
up some precious time, I come home and cry.
Matthew, dear friend, the Passion ends in tears:

Sleep well  Gather strength  Get to Paris
Complete the Camus   Abide with us
as long as you can  When the time comes
*Ruhe sanfte, sanfte ruh'!*

## BLACK STONES VIII

(And were You lost, I would be—)


Paralyzed in the face
powerless how
to face your death (better
prepared than most)
dissolving at the thought
more frequent now

At thirty-nine you may
be gone   Maybe
before   I who know stop
hoping now in
secret for miracles
remedy cure

Today I am wholly
tears:  desire
to keep you here   Who am
I to suggest
any given day should
not be your last?

I have to translate all
your wordless fear
and pain into my own—
again:  blankness—
Death's mask devours my face
Like Gretel take

your hand but the woods close
all around and

everything feeds on you
even our
father
          Beyond reason
caution I love

you selfishly   Rush in
where demons have
the floor   We share more than
I'll ever care
to analyze   Time was
writing preserved

anesthetized carried
me somewhere safe
No refuge—here   Only
tears   Sustenance
Colorless substance of
Despair

## For Elisabeth

What do I mean to tell you, you at six,
child not mine, the one child I will have?
Why do I need to write you in this book
of horrors—illness, death? You who dance
through your fevers, ask, at a funeral, if
the dead in their private boxes must wear
clothes, muse afterward: so many old folks,
there must be thousands more underground.
So unlike the child I was at your age.

Am now. With thirty years between us, you
insist that until I have a kid, I'll
be one. . . . By *kid* I guess you mean a state
of mind, of play, a gift for entering
someone else's imagination (yours).
Or is it merely, spoiling godmother
that I am, I rarely scold or forbid
anything but sweets at 10 A.M.?

Elisabeth, I love you, love how you
beg me to stay on longer than I plan,
love the sound of your voice on my phone tape
saying, "Rika, [kiss, kiss, kiss, kiss] when
are you coming next?" Love how your love asks
nothing but that I play.
                         I've missed half of
your birthdays, sick with a sickness I pray you
will never know.
                Happy child, how old will
you grow before you read this book? I grew
up with my nose in books, my mother's illness
before my shielded but seeing eyes,

the weight of it pressing the life out of
my life, which, as someday you'll learn, I
have tried to take.
                The gift I would like to
make you (for once not pink doughnuts, heart-shaped
stickers or soap, paper fans, or tiny
dinosaurs) is the hope and the knowledge:
*The worst does pass and can be survived.*

Summer's child, camp is over. Your mom says
two of your front teeth are loose. My mind's eye
blinks: You are prone on your bed, kicking up
your heels, wearing a bra and god-knows-what
kind of post-punk hairdo, talking for hours
and hours on the phone . . . to me I hope,
planning the trip to Sweden I promised
you at four, or calling to say: "Rika,
I just read that book of yours, you know,
the one with *Hell* in the title. It's alright,
I love you. All right, that is, except for
the poem about me. What made you think I
was so happy?"

                You did. Your joy was
contagious. It was your gift to me.

*1989*

# BLACK STONES XII

(Care)

The ill can tyrannize
Needing care demanding
care protesting they don't
want it   Some in despair
would sooner die than ask

(I know this well: Once I
pulled threats like ropes around
the throats of those closest
to me   Ask myself still:
*Why did they not flee? What*
*binds us—love or duty?*)

Helpless irate mostly
oblivious they clutch
and flail all but consume
us   Seizing control through
what they can withhold—
a word a look a kiss
Only a mother's love
survives this

            And we
attend them trembling
and blind uncertain how
much to do when not to

Love that adheres that clings
in the end disables
the sick and the well
Not an abandoning
this letting go

Past love's  
calling care is *lament*  
*grief sorrow*

# BLACK STONES  XIV

### (Past tense)

It's over   You're
over   You died
here   In the end
you could not did
not want to go
Your corpse alone
flew to Denver
I did not see
you that last week:
briefly vital
then finally
sunken holding
your mother's and
your sister's hands
saying *Don't leave*

When you left I
was bleeding had
cut my hand on
a jagged tin
felt nothing mind
empty body
numb yet somehow
aware   Pouring
rain   New Haven
Elisabeth
turning seven:
*Gremlins 2*, I
couldn't watch the
gory bits   She

could   You would have
loved this teased me
mercilessly

Hardest of all:
letting the small
things go   One day
in St. Luke's you
asked me to turn
away from you
the near-naked
body I'd held
cradled lifted
from bed to chair
days before—*You're
squeamish, Rika
—Matthew, I am
beyond that now*
Holding you help-
less in great pain
was (my mind was
wordless then) was
sacramental

Was and was   The
past tense is hard
to use   You are
under the earth
wearing your French
green linen suit
The glossy black
circles of your
eyeglass frames glare
toward the lid of
not quite the plain

146

pine coffin you
wanted
   I want
to respect your
wishes honor
your memory
will not forget
the order you
gave me on my
last birthday and
again when once
I had to leave:
*Rika, dear friend,*
*live and live and live!*

## The Other Life

It is not the work of art you make
It is yourself
　　　　—Gunnar Ekelöf, "Ex Ponto"
You cannot
enter into any bond and
be free of it
　　　　—Göran Sonnevi


*How was it this time?*

Too brief. After seventeen years, more
than a word-hoard unlocks. In four weeks
links—friends present and former loves and
associations—go critical,
unleash a chain reaction that can't
be contained in time. Time enough to
revive the other language, not to
resume the other life.

*Why Sweden in the first place?*

God knows, the choice was arbitrary.
I was sick of German and tired of
interpreting. At Yale, having dropped
Organic Chem and put all my eggs
in the Literature Basket,
I felt a crack. Gluing mind and soul
together demanded going back
to rote, learning things by heart. Language
study, first of all, means commitment
to rules, keeping oneself within lines,
not reading between them. Call it a

"rage for order." Experiments—like
living abroad—came later.

*And you liked living there?*

I wouldn't say that, for many years
it was more an ambivalence. I
landed with the language but against
the currents and grain of the culture.
1974: Göteborg
(a port, the second largest city)
was insular, hostile, and anti-
American. There is a term, not
in the lexicons, to describe those
swarthy of complexion or of hair:
*svartskallar,* it's used for unwanted
immigrants, unwelcome *Gastarbeiter.*
Technically not one of them, I still
belonged nowhere, left the Department
dumbfounded because—except to note
some *ibid* should read *op cit*—no one
spoke in seminars. Inside silence
reigned, outside it poured; trained to speak
my mind, I was becoming a sleeping
Fury. Best to stay home alone, stay
up all night, as Ekelöf prescribed.
Then, at least, the sky, diurnally
skull-gray, went black as my hair; only
then, *"ensam i tysta Natten,"* could
I work calmly, faculties clear.

*And yet you returned repeatedly.*

I went as a sleepwalker, blindly,
oblivious. A small voice urged: *Face*

*the silence, contend with intervals*
*of displacement, loss of your mother*
*tongue.*  I can't say when this laconic,
taciturn people made me their own.
(Perhaps I had reinstated home
away from home.)

                  Without blood ties I'm
still a mystery.  From Ekelöf
to Sonnevi, correspondences
have been subjective, arbitrary.


Over lunch years ago (not *gravad*
*lax* but sushi) here in New York, my
favorite editor asked me, *Rika,*
*when you speak Swedish or German, are*
*you a different person?*  Something must
have slipped out—I had not yet learned
to hold my tongue—like "Swedes hardly speak
to anyone." Thinking, silently,
*Yes, I am,* but did not mean to be.


                    *Silent or split?*


Keeping silence is a decision
and a tool; self-division is not
wholly within one's control.  Only
this last year or so have I felt one
and the same wherever.  Surprises
do come:

                Hässelby Strand in August,
guest in an apartment of a friend
of a friend, one whose walls of windows
opened on Mälaren, I would rise
with the sun to see what the lake was
doing. Waves? The shape and texture of
clouds perched closer at high latitude?

Göran and I worked there afternoons.
Where was I? Or was that *who*? A New
Yorker, still? I, ecstatic to be
peripheral, forty minutes from
the suck and whorl of central Stockholm!

*Did you go elsewhere?*

Oh yes, to pick mushrooms once or twice,
just where is secret, of course. And to
Sigtuna. Nine years past the time I
turned up unannounced—so nervous, three
times I circled the Ekelöf house
before finding it! Ingrid likes to
play the recluse. This day, so it turned
out, was her daughter's birthday. Suzanne,
a scant year older than I, her son
Marcus, thirteen (they live in Aix), Ingrid
about eighty, three generations . . .

*You were happy then?*

I could not shake Grief, damned flatfoot, blood-
hound from Hell. 1990 goes down
an Inferno year:
                    Mary Sandbach—
Strindberg-translator, dear oldest friend
at eighty-nine—was dying. I would
not see her at her daughter's party
in Gamla Stan or out for a stroll
down Kammakargatan. Now she's gone,
died at home in Cambridge this autumn.
I hear her voice, the laugh that puckered
her massively wrinkled face. That she
was old does not make her end hurt less.

Back in my old stomping grounds, home in
exile—the East River my Black Sea;
both tongues Greek to me, I'll tie the roots,
declare *ex ponto* from the Bridge, Hart's
"harp and altar." (We share a birthday.)
Home at work, at home in pain, making
myself over again:
                The Human
Bridge—her cables and strings of fury
resonate; of flesh, most tenuous
link and briefest span; restless *enjambe-*
*ment*, unable to set her feet down
invariably on either side.

Where will this lead? Where would I like to
be? I'm not sure the answer is mine.
"Art is deep uncertainty." (That last
word also means "insecurity";
Gunnar, peace.) I will tread softly, soul
and body bound wherever the tide
of my heart's blood, rising and falling,
carries me.

# PAGES TOWARD THE TURN OF THE YEAR

*Men are*

> largely absent from this book
though not entirely, there's
> my father
> my mother's father
>> (my father's father left the household when my dad and
>> uncle were young; we children saw him rarely, called him
>> Big Grandpa; died 1970, hit by a car whose driver left
>> the scene)
> the ones who dare not call unless drunk
> my mom's psychiatrist
> Matthew, of course (not straight)
> the wretch who inspired me last spring to write a poem called
>> "Shrinking" (now part of this text)
> the one I fell in and out of love with, unable to care for anyone
> but himself

But aren't they *all* like that (indulge me, right now I can't afford
> to qualify) lacking some quality of caring or of love, the
> ability, desire, imagination to change places with anyone?
>> (Who would, still, in this world, with a woman?)

Or is something wrong with me?
> Intelligent, even beautiful many now say
>> (I trust when I hear this from my women friends)
> honest (not always a plus), faithful, brave . . .

Why am I not "involved" with any one?

Something to do with major past gutting flames?

A–B C:  Swedish, 15 years older than I, the jealous type—I never
got my own keys to his Gothenburg flat

D E F:  Vietnam vet, great in bed, wanted to marry me, but not
bright enough, and apt to go off, a time bomb

G HI:  Half-Jewish, zany, a painter who turned his talents to
making money and topographic maps; just as I learned to
trust him, he turned on me

J K:  Full-blooded Jew, super-intense, interests: music and
math, problem: mediocrity

An alphabet soup of lower flames that burned:
    the body flaring up in desire, consuming
    the mind funnelling ashes into urns

Lastly, the man I cannot hate enough, the one I call, in polite
    conversation,

## Bad Male Shrink

> . . . that
> we can't predict what
> our actions will lead to
> absolves us, tho not
> altogether: . . .
>
> —A. R. Ammons
> *Tape for the Turn of the Year*, 7 Dec:


Let's call him Dr. H or Dr. Hearse, transferred to after my first
    attempt; at first he seemed humane, compassionate
A poor dermatologist is unlikely to do much harm, but a bad shrink
    can be a mortal danger
I remember Dr. H once asking me (he'd prescribed pills for my insomnia)
    —You're not going to kill yourself, are you?
    —No, well, not this week!
I remember: Second time in the hospital, calling him from D.C.
    —Help me get out of here, please!
    —How big is the ward, I mean, in square feet?
At their wits' end, the team at Payne Whitney declared
    —Dr. Hearse has absented himself from your case


I've dreamed about torching his office, stealing his book . . .
Catching sight of him on the street
    (he works *and* lives in my neighborhood!)
        I invent retorts:
            —Still practicing? You still need to
                —I'm fine thanks, no thanks to you
Language, my sword, help me to finish him!
I keep tormenting myself with my part in this:


One day I heard an alarm I dared not heed:
    —You don't care about me as a person, I said on the phone,
        meaning exactly that, *a human being*

His reply: audible irritation, nervous cough
                    I knew in his head he'd heard "woman"
Highly verbal, could I have talked him into believing I was sane?
I tried to keep faith, desperately needed to ... grew hostile ...
          sought to appease him with half-truths ...
Severely depressed, working my way toward paranoid psychosis, I could
          tune in, read minds (at times these readings were confirmed);
                    his transmitted: *Get away from me, you bitch!*
No, in retrospect, his knack for not taking me at my word when I was
          *dead serious* was clearly malicious

What have I learned from this?
          My subsequent shrinks have been female
          It is unwise to trust blindly, especially when ill, to entrust
                    your living soul to any physician or individual

*10 December 1990*

> plenty of food & water in
> paradise but some
>   confusion about sex:
> anything so sweet
> should come hard
> as bread & water:
>             —A. R. Ammons
> *Tape for the Turn of the Year,* 9 Dec:


After a weekend away—D.C.: Titian, Van Dyke, and friends' new babies—
good to be in my own bed again, aloft, a fearsome height to some men I've
been with, a delight to others, although they must sleep on the edge,
the side with no wall

Out of different times and different mouths:
     —Great to be inside you—some women are too tight, others are
       too loose
     —I had no idea you'd be so athletic
     —I'm afraid I won't satisfy you
     —Get that stuffed animal out of bed!
     —*Tycker du inte om att älska?*
     —Isn't there always some pain involved?
     —You sleep like a statue
                  Stony silence
                        Soft silence
                              Touch alone

Lately, sleeping with bears, remembering someone I wish were here
     I think, like an animal, about having a mate
But having just been with infants (all weekend I called Margaret's Ania
      "Little Mammal"), happy moms, forbearing dads who looked soft
      and proud but somehow excluded

I know it's not a child I want
The man who is not here (yes, another Swede) might do—
    he had the touch
    of someone who loves women

Meanwhile, when unprotected by gay friends, I elude tall dark young things
    who stalk at parties, drinks in hand, mouths spilling talk not of mak-
    ing art but the wherewithal to acquire it: —Too bad I couldn't
    *buy* Strindberg's sketches two years ago . . . Circles are small, again
    we meet, eye each other, do not speak

Horny tonight, I entertain the thought:
    Locked up for a week with an attractive beast
    would I screw him, just like that?

                                Nowadays, probably not
I want more than *that*

But sometimes the body succumbs, as it does to illness:

## Shrinking

I see a woman shrinking, shrinking
     (I don't know what he sees)
physically only   Inside she is bound-
less, open, more knowing than ever
     (I don't know who he sees)

*I want you, he says, wanted you badly*
*at first sight—you can't know how much*
     (I am a woman rapidly shrinking,
     my body laid out like cloth)
Pinned down under him, I register, mark

his every move, his lines   Out of love,
this first time in months feels odd, an X
movie, an off-Broadway farce
     (Making love to myself
     through a stranger's eyes—
     a narcissistic exercise?)

Younger than he, in years at least, I burn
with luminous calm   The smaller I grow,
the sexier . . . a beacon for lost
boys   What have their fathers done, not done
that they should know nothing of touch?

Can they love us, wanting nothing
but the mothers they have lost?   Bodi-
less women, icon and no longer flesh,
eidolon   Skin and bones only, I crack,
recoil, shrinking from his touch

## 11 December

How to write about men?  I've never understood them
Seen through them, yes, loved some, been bored, hurt, disappointed,
        furious, bored
Strange creatures always saying, rarely in so many words:
                Look at me
                Look at what I've done
                Admire and
                      Praise
When not Competition or Someone Else to them
  one may be stroked occasionally in return

Not part of my youth in almost any form:
      A house full of women (Mom and Us Three Girls)
      A hardworking father neither absent nor there:
           the latch on the bedroom door meant *Let me work*
                                *in peace*

I just learned a friend with many sibs is bulimic, says her food and
        sex issues got tangled as she vied for her father's attention
           Her father (a doctor who fed her diet pills) is dead
Mine, a man of science, who cared for, treated my mother
      in sickness (unforgettable: her long rambling word-strings,
              weeping, wailing, wandering through the house)
      and    (of which, after electroshock, she recalled
           almost nothing)
    in health
          as though she were a bird who loved her cage . . .
Trust him?
      I held him in contempt
                was not allowed
                      to show it

Most of my life I've understood nothing but tone

These last few years the family has been taking lessons,
       learning to speak
    in words

## 18 December

Same old loop: telling the body's
from the mind's possible illness
To what end? Damned if I do; damned
sick last week—lithium level
checked—a virus indeed had caused
headaches and nausea, I turned
on Astrid and her hard disk crashed!
Backed-up but heart-sunk after long
tests, I replaced it. Now, if not
a Hardware Queen, I'm a Princess.
Joyful or distressed, this body
craves systems diagnostics that
will reformat suspect sectors
in memory, find bad clusters,
mark them, display: NO DANGER, at
least report: HEAD SELECT ERROR,
INCORRECTLY INSTALLED HEART

*Christmas Day*

Started rereading Ammons's long skinny poem last night, who knows how many more feet of adding-machine tape I have to go, I'm on page 120 or so. No entries for Christmas eve or day. . . . Some strange ahas, akin to his "saliences."

When he wrote *Tape*, he was my age, also a smoker, and unemployed. Cornell took him. (They once took me, the would-be biochemist, but then I got off Yale's waiting list. I've often wondered if, in Ithaca, I would have remained in the Sciences, or studied with Ammons, ending up much the same as I am.)

Stranger still: The way he records what he observes in nature, the course and discourse of his scientific mind, his writing on Eros—all resemble Sonnevi's. Now and then, in different contexts of course, they have written the same lines.

Even the weather patterns—December lightning, too-warm days followed by cold—are in accord. And this morning, in the bare linden tree, a jay.

## Questions of Love

        if we were at the
        mercy of what
        we understand,
        our eyes couldn't see:
             —A. R. Ammons
        *Tape for the Turn of the Year,* 31 Dec:

What did I want from them, or they from me,
not just the "men" but the "boys" at school?
Surely not merely physical pleasure—
At age five I discovered masturbation (nameless then)—
      it took some years of late teen-age experience to realize
    men could bestow the pleasure I had alone

Never did learn how to flirt, how to be jealous, dig in my claws,
        hang on (or out)
Only approach I knew (still suffer from) was as an equal
Have lived both sides of seduction, not much fun
All I want is a close friend who's good in bed
        Unheard-of? Too utopian?

So ends the worst year of my life:
Alone still, but hale and sane and fully human
Maybe I could have done more for my departed friends, but
        at no prior time could I have loved them more

My seven-year-old goddaughter (in public school she
    defends how to say my name) informs me now:
        *Rika, you know, you're half a kid (Quit pinching my bears!)*
        *and half a grown-up (Dieting today?)*
Do I want to grow *all the way?*

May the new year bring new leaves, better times
Resolved, in the interim:

      To be adult:  severing attachments that no longer serve
      To be childlike:  trusting those I love will never leave

## September '92: Measures

Fats, sweets, thick dairy, eggplant in olive oil
Cigarettes, a pipe, Nicorette, gradually bumming all
Fear of movement, missteps, exertion, injury
These I gave up over two years
somewhat uneasily—smoking  died
hard   In their place
Nautilus, acupuncture, NordicTrack, free weights
And in May we began to lower my lithium
slowly   Three months I wept
for the old diagnoses
*Bipolar u*, my shrink calls me now (meaning "unspecified")
a term of affection, I feel—even if medical   *She* needs
this kind of language
I give up her fear I'll become manic, my own of becoming de-
pressed
the rational desire, at times, not to exist
at this point in history
I give up my father's demand everything be verifiable scientifically
my mother's belief new miseries await us each day
I give up carrying messages
the compulsion to translate
other people's work   Look
at me   I have ceased
hiding   Here
I am

I give up hating my parents, though sometimes I'll scold them
for bringing me into the world
*What were you thinking?* I ask
I love them despite their blindness for their blindness   Don't know
what else to call this feeling after all these years

That so much of life is ridiculous arbitrary
so many years have been wasted are wasted—inevitably?—time and
again in family after family birth after birth
no matter how much LOVE is assumed or declared   There
is so much misery   It is so powerful it kills heedlessly
many more than it challenges   I have seen this with my own eyes
I have been only one mirror   One pair of crazed
eyes—splintered yet intact—returned from the world of glass


If it were mine
                    to start again from
                                                    the beginning
to choose the time
                              the place
                                                  the life
I would change
                    just about everything
                                                        It is not


                    So I choose
                    to lie down beside
                    what was my
                    illness   Face to face
                    memorize
                    its features   Then stand
                    up erect
                    very relaxed with
                    poise with grace
                    And walk
                    away from it

N

**Etruscan**

I  A Handle on Things                              Degli Sposi  XII

III  The Warning                                    Final Questions  X

IV  Sarcophagus                                      Hut Urn  VII

XII  From Vetulonia                          The Mummy Speaks  I

*Pars Dextra (Hostilis)*

*Pars Sinistra (Familiaris)*

**Things**

**1978–1981**

S

## A Handle on Things

Molded into a shape the hand
wants to hold,
the smooth bronze of a body
in miniature:

> My head rests on the blade,
> hair and neck stiff, arms bent
> back and raised, my body, a girl's
> body lets you use an incense shovel.

> Stout warriors, we twin brothers
> gaze past our beards, bear
> his weight on opposite arms:
> Our spears cannot prod him
> to life. May Charun not raise
> his hammer above this youth's
> fair head.

> Broken off from our objects
> we wrestle, offer
> libations, perform
> acrobatics, blow the curved
> horn, dance with satyrs, embrace
> one another's shoulders.
> *Embrace* as Tages ordered
> when he gave the Law to Tarchon.

*Touch us. Hold us. Keep us.*
What we were attached to
lost long ago.

## The Warning

The difference between us and the Etruscans. . . is the
following: whereas we believe lightning to be released as
a result of the collision of clouds, they believe clouds collide
so as to release lightning.  For as they attribute all to the deity,
they are led to believe not that things have a meaning in so far as
they occur, rather that they occur because they must have a meaning.
—Seneca,  *Quaestiones naturales* II. 32. 2.

Open or closed my eyes
are blind.  Blinded and
hollow, like shells empty
of eggs.  My lips—slightly
parted—frozen, seared
shut.  They want to let out
a cry: a cavernous
O.  But what I saw
would not let me be
myself, troubled my
worship, made me strike
this pose.

Into my right hand
the lightning fell.
A bolt from Tinia—
it was red—I'm sure.
It glittered before
it burned and hardened
me.  Was it the first
of three, the one he
hurls at will?

My sisters in worship form
a ring at my feet. But now
they beat their breasts, hands
over hearts, mourning: for me?
I raised my left hand up
toward my mouth, to stifle
its cry, cover its grimace.

The lightning slipped through
my fingers. They wrap
around Nothing now;
my thumb still points to
the sky. I was not
quick enough to see
where the clouds clashed.
Was it his second bolt—
of harm and good—cast
by consent of the Twelve
Great Gods?

Below the first ring of mourners,
a second, but here animals
join in: long necks of shrieking
gryphons, beaks open wide. They
saw it coming, too, were struck
the same as I.

The third bolt may be
thrown only by the grace
of the Nameless Ones.
It annihilates all
it touches, changes
the course of mankind.

I am not, as some say, a deity
of death. The force of the gods
shot through me, turned me into
a monument guarding charred bones.
the meaning the clay I am embodies:

> *O my people, I tell you*
> *to change your lives.*

## Sarcophagus

Even in life my lover
said: "You sleep like a statue,
not like most people—curled up
animals."

       I can still see
the Day of Parting—perhaps
more clearly from inside this
box. At my feet, on the stone,
the journey takes form. Out there
stand two of me, one on each
side of my brother. Behind
him I touch his shoulder, bid
farewell. Before him I am
veiled, untouchable.

Dream scenes enclose me. The long recurrent
ones fret my two sides. Caught between beasts
a hart in pain: lion claws scrape his thigh,
fangs tear into his rump. The hart does
not struggle, cranes his neck, closes one eye.
A beak slashes his throat; the gryphon's
tail, a snake arched back to strike, peers into
Charun's eyes. The demon—casual,
hypnotized—leans on the hammer he has
no need to raise. His serpent hand poised,
Tuchulca looks on, down his snout, wanting
the lion's share. . . . This much I have learned:
we creatures spoil ourselves. There is nothing
more to fear.

At my head—
dead reckoning: two Lasas
record my deeds on tablets,
on scrolls. What's done—
is done.

My right hand clasps a pomegranate whose
crimson pulp disintegrates even now;
white seeds line its comb of cells, the rind—dark
as dried blood—complete. My left hand, folded
under my cheek, has fallen asleep. I
offer myself to the stone network of
tiny mouths. . . . Above the empty space my
flesh no longer fills, my being hovers,
settles, forms a lid. As in life, I rest
there—alone—on a hard, unquiet bed.

## From Vetulonia

These cannot speak for themselves
so I'll speak for them,
Bound to each other with a triple chain:

> found loose in the earth
> above a circular tomb,
> a man and his woman, roughly
> four inches high.  He,
> a head taller, stands a short
> distance from her, needn't
> lift a finger to keep her
> within range.

> Their elliptical heads angle
> back, jaws project; ears,
> round and flat, cling to the long,
> thick necks.  In profile like axeheads
> rising out of two bundles of rods:  even
> more like apes' skulls—beasts
> from the neck up;

> down below

> her broad shoulders, high
> on her narrow chest, small,
> rounded, prominent breasts.  Her arms
> corset her ribcage.  His, caught
> in the chain, are suppressed.

> The bronze links run
> from the end of her braid
> to his elbows, almost graze

the tip of his large, erect
phallus. She leans forward;
her knees are locked. He holds
himself upright by tilting back.

Seen from one side, the coupling
is terribly clear: with no chain
between them, they'd be inseparable.

# The Mummy Speaks

Mummy of a young woman (with wrappings removed)
standing in a glass case and held upright by an iron rod.
Another glass case contains the mummy's bandages which
are completely covered with writing in an unknown and
hitherto undeciphered language . . .

What did you take me for, Michael
Baric, that day in Alexandria
in eighteen hundred forty-eight?
Did you expect to be taken?  Palmed off
with a bundle of sticks, rubbish,
sawdust, cats' skeletons, stuffed by human
hand into a non-human skin
in the back street of a Cairo bazaar?
Even my case is real. You set
it on end in your salon, telling
the credulous ladies it held
the sister of King Stephen
of Hungary! You never looked
inside.  Later, you died, left me
to your brother, Elias, pastor
in some godforsaken Slavonian
village.  He reviled me, packed me off
to Agram, where they dishoused, stripped
and catalogued me: "an outstanding
treasure of the National Museum."

The iron rod eats into what little
flesh I have left. And I'm cold.
Cold comfort my words, unstrung
In a case nearby.

*ceia hia . . .*
*ceia hia etnam ciz vacl trin velthre*

And the linguists who came to visit
not me, but my wrappings: Herr Doktor
Heinrich Brugsch, and that beastly
Sir Richard Burton! *Narren*, fools,
I say, thinking my words, my letters,
"partly Greco-European and
partly Runic," or Arabic
translation from the Book of the Dead.

*male ceia hia etnam ciz vacl aisvale*
*male ceia hia trinth etnam ciz ale*

More than one man of the cloth has laid
hands on me. The museum director,
the abbé Ljubic removed my bandages
to his study, but not before he'd
dispensed great lengths of them to his
congregation. Scattering the gods
whose wills they could not read. And here
I shrivel, my toes curl, my chin—
sharp as a knife—cuts my sternum.

*male ceia hia etnam ciz vacl vile vale*

What nonsense I have heard these many
years through the transparent walls
of this rigid case! Even a man of
instinct, Jacob Krall, could not take
my words at face value, took them
first to Vienna, suspecting the ink,
the linen of forgery. When he was
sure—my words are Etruscan—

I was cross-examined:
—Is she Egyptian?
—Why bury a book with a girl?
—Is she Etruscan?
—Why wind the strips so that the writing touches her flesh?

*staile itrile hia ciz trinthaśa śacnitn*

They photographed my words under
infrared light, made transcriptions,
exposed them to questioning eyes.
Trying to trace my words through tangled
roots, who sought to render them
fell into deepest night. One heard cries
rising from the cloth. Another saw
sacrifice to a vulture god. I danced
before them: a witch, a troll, or served
my ancestors an insubstantial meal.

Have they considered that without me
The text has no meaning? Our language
was reserved: we spoke only among
ourselves. Is this why they parted us:
afraid I would take every sign
away from them? The bitumen that
seeped through my skin and into the cloth
transformed the words. They entered my flesh,
became whole inside me. Black ink on
white cloth: opaque remains. The meanings
lie in the lacunae.

## Hut Urn

So deep in the earth,
below layers of ash, of tufa,
you might never find me,
but for the tumulus:

That huge mound of earth
—girded by stones,
on a stone base—
mimics my roof.

Open my door.  In the gable
peer through the smokehole.  Inside
I am dark as the artificial cave
you entered searching for me.

The house *is* the body I tell you.
I am the house of fired clay.
I hold the ashes of the woman
who lived in a hut of daubed clay.

The tombs plough their way underground,
below that perishable earthen roof.
The stone mouth narrows,
recedes, disintegrates.
                    Out of reach
I hold myself whole.

# Final Questions

Is the route safe? Why
this armed guide, a wingless
guardian with thick thighs,
a bow, two naked arrows? Why
this haste? Won't our goal
last?

Putting your soul
into another's hands—
no easy matter.
Of spirit alone,
he may not know, may
not care to hold you
without hurting you
out of harm's way. How
to carry you (where?).
He runs too swiftly.
The wings at his ankles
blur.

I watch my body walk
away from me.
Swarthy companions—
one bears a spear—
surround, enfold,
encompass her.

Maybe I am safe, am saved
and the path is clear.
It is not a man in whose
arms I am snared, but
Artemis, appeased.

The air we travel
cradles us.

O Mother, take me
to safety.
To certainty.

## Degli Sposi

Of us
not much is known.
Our lives were not
extraordinary.
Our silence seals
a deeper silence.

Sharing the single bed, how close
we lie; fingers curved over palms
whose fable reads: *conjugal bliss
is possible.*

How simple it was.  It is.
But the secret's lost.  That's why
you look to us, how we carry
ourselves, our smile.  We live
in that space where all's yet
to become: embrace—a tenderness,
an expectation, myth, tentative
gesture preceding touch.  Before
the shock of contact, when caution
counsels:  Leave.

Not at all easy, this, to speak
of love.  And to survive.  Our skin
glows red with passion in reserve.
Unbridled, it would deaden every
nerve.  Feeling—the reins, the check,
restraint, repose, out of whose thousand
fragments we are restored.  Loving
each other even after death.  As if
life were not, had not been, enough.

We touch, we hold, we keep
one another free.

# Chronology and Notes

The source for the first sonnet from *Astrophel and Stella* is an unauthorized first quarto published in 1591 by Thomas Newman. I have modernized the spelling and punctuation.

QUESTIONS OF LOVE

QUESTIONS OF LOVE, RECONSIDERED
The poems that comprise this sequence were composed between the summer of 2002 and Boxing Day, 2005.

ABOUT HER
Dates of completion for the poems in the book's mid-section range more widely, from the summer of 1996 to the autumn of 2005.

THE GIRLS were created between the summer of 2002 and the last day of 2005 in response to the works of Lena Cronqvist, except for "Self-Portraits: Reflections—Letters to Lena," written during the spring/summer of 2006 for the catalogue of her New York show at the Nancy Margolis Gallery in the fall.

Cronqvist (b. 1938) is a renowned Swedish artist whose paintings, sculptures, and graphics have been shown widely in Scandinavia, as well as Brazil, China, Egypt, France, the United States, and elsewhere. She was elected a member of The Royal Swedish Academy of Fine Arts in 1997; in 2002 she received a Carnegie Art Award. Her "girls" (Swedish *flickorna*) date mainly from the 1990s to the present, though some (the three paintings *The Ice, The Road, The Hedge*) date from the mid-1970s. Her 1971-canvas *The Experiences Being Painted Over* appeared, alarmingly reproduced, on the cover of *All We Need of Hell*.

*Samling Saltarvet*, the Saltarvet Collection, also known as the Saltarvet Hall of Art, opened in Bohuslän's Fiskebäckskil in June 2005. It consists of Studio Lena Cronqvist, a permanent base displaying selections from her private collection as well as Separat

Saltarvet, rooms in which to show temporary exhibitions of contemporary Swedish artists from its own base holdings.

**"With Poppies"**: I had two particular paintings in my mind's eye: *Girl, Poppy, and Gorilla*, tempera on canvas, 1992, and *The Red Poppy*, oil on canvas, 1984.

**"In a Bottle"**: The Swedish verb *dra (draga)* is cognate with German *tragen*, and English "draw." One can "draw" a cork out of a bottle. One can say *"det drar"* ("there's a draft") of a room with a draft or of a chimney, of steeping tea, or of something which pulls you toward it.

**"Standing Meditation"**: The *nalle* in this poem is a teddy bear, not a cell phone. Reading on the web about Animal Frolics (Wu Qin Xi) Qigong, particularly the Bear Frolic, I came across the following: "The Bear has been revered as the great Medicine Chief throughout the Northern Hemisphere for thousands of years. Traditional societies have honored the Bear as ancestor, keeper of herbal lore, sacred archetype of motherhood and rebirth, powerful protector, and messenger of the return of spring." —Margaret Duperly, *The Power of Bear Spirit*

**"Self-Portraits: Reflections—Letters to Lena"**:
*Göran Tunström* (1937-2000) celebrated and beloved Swedish novelist, Tunström and Cronqvist married in 1964.
*Gunnar Ekelöf* (1907-1968) perhaps the greatest lyric poet Sweden produced in the second half of the 20th century, his works have been translated into English by W. H. Auden, Muriel Ruykeser, myself, and others. (See also "Losses" among the Selected Poems.)

## SELECTED POEMS

In the "Commentary and Notes" to *Growing Back*, published more than a decade ago, I gave a chronological account of the contents of my earlier books of poetry, and I wrote about their interrelationship to the works of three poets I have translated, namely Rilke, Ekelöf, and Sonnevi. Because I had published *Etruscan Things*, a through-composed volume, before the more urgent lifeline *All We Need of*

*Hell*, it wasn't until *Growing Back* that I published an ordinary "collection." Even that omitted quite a few poems from what had been my Scholar of the House thesis at Yale (1974) and my masters thesis at Columbia School of the Arts (1977), the latter entitled *Blueprints and Monuments.*

When Stanley Moss invited me to present *Questions of Love* as a New and Selected volume (and to reprint *Etruscan Things* separately), I disinterred some earlier poems. Here is some further history, or perhaps archaeology.

## FIRST POEMS

Most of these poems were written between my sophomore and senior years at Yale.

"The News & The Weather" was the first poem I published nationally, in *American Review* 18. When "The Room" came out in *American Review* 21 in 1974, I received the first David Oliker Award.

"Ein Geliebtes" appeared first in *Holding Out*, my first book, a selection of Rilke's poetry, published as one of Harry Duncan's rare and splendid Abattoir Editions in 1975, before it was reprinted in 1986 by Princeton under the title *Rilke: Between Roots.* Both books are out of print.

"Rika Lesser" has been fussed with since 1974, but it belongs with these other poems. As a Yale Scholar of the House, I wrote and translated poetry (and continued to learn Swedish) during my senior year, while Paul Zelinsky was mainly painting in oils on canvas. He is much better known nowadays, with an O. between Paul and Zelinsky, for myriad gorgeous or amusingly illustrated books for children of all ages.

## BLUEPRINTS AND MONUMENTS

All but three of these poems are in *Growing Back*, though here "The Gifts" appears in a longer variant. "Menorah," "Under the Weather," and "Eight Days a Week," have never before been published. Excluding "CAN ZONE . . . ," which dates from October 1983, the poems were written between June 1974 and April 1979. The painting described in "Under the Weather" is one by Paul Zelinsky.

## ALL WE NEED, AND MORE

All these poems except for "PAGES TOWARD THE TURN OF THE YEAR" (1990 into 1991) come from *All We Need of Hell* and date from 1986-1992. With the inclusion of "PAGES ..." here, the poems are now arranged in chronological order of composition. The unit of composition for "PAGES ..." (first printed in *Growing Back*) was the capacious A4 journal page, allowing for long, unbroken, and non-wrapping lines, far more easily mimicked on 8 ½ x 11-inch paper than in the diminutive pages of this book itself. I want to thank the Press for working with me where linear rearrangement was necessary. Finally, Astrid, my desktop computer in the "18 December" section, was an AST Premium 286.

## ETRUSCAN THINGS

These poems date from the summer of 1978 to the summer of 1981. The first four are from the book's *Pars Dextra (Hostilis)* and the second from the *Pars Sinistra (Familiaris)*, the Etruscans having everything properly reversed. Women enjoyed equality with men, or perhaps it was the other way around. Proceed around the circular contents, based on the scheme in the book itself, which contains 24 poems, in a counter-clockwise direction.

**Rika Lesser** is the author of three earlier collections of poetry, *Etruscan Things* (Braziller, 1983), *All We Need of Hell* (North Texas, 1995), and *Growing Back* (South Carolina, 1997). She has translated and published collections of poetry by Göran Sonnevi, Gunnar Ekelöf, and Claes Andersson, as well as Rainer Maria Rilke and Hermann Hesse (including *Siddhartha: An Indic Poem*, Barnes & Noble Classics, 2007). She has been the recipient of the Amy Lowell Traveling Poetry Scholarship, fellowships from the Fulbright Foundation and the National Endowment for the Arts, the Poetry Translation Prize of the Swedish Academy, as well as other awards. She teaches poetry and literary translation and has long made Brooklyn Heights her home.